A Conversation with
Dick, the Dagger

Chaffcutter Books

The Society for Sailing Barge Research

The Society for Spritsail Barge Research was established in 1963 by a band of enthusiasts concerned that the rapid decline and possible extinction of these splendid and historically significant craft would pass largely unrecorded. From the thousands of Thames sailing barges once plying the estuaries of the south-east and beyond, today just a handful survive in active commission, charter parties and business guests replacing the grain, cement and coal cargoes of yesteryear.

Now renamed The Society for Sailing Barge Research, reflecting a broadening interest in other allied types of craft, the Society organises walks, talks and exhibitions and publishes Topsail, a regular treasure chest of sailing barge history profusely illustrated with fascinating photographs of long lost craft and the ports they once served. Members also receive a twice yearly newsletter which highlights the fortunes of those barges which survive, as well as providing further snippits of our maritime heritage as ongoing research yields yet more of that trade, a way of life which from origins going back hundreds, even thousands of years, ceased in 1970 when the *Cambria* carried her last freight under sail alone.

Membership enquiries to Margaret Blackburn,
21 Newmarket Road, Stretham, Cambridgeshire CB6 3JZ

Published by
CHAFFCUTTER BOOKS
39 Friars Road, Braughing, Ware, Hertfordshire SG11 2NN, England

© Tony Farnham and various authors 2001

THE BRITISH LIBRARY CATALOGUING IN PUBLICATION DATA:
A CATALOGUE RECORD FOR THIS BOOK IS AVAILABLE FROM THE BRITISH LIBRARY

(First published as ISBN 0-9500515-8-6 in 2001 by the Society for Sailing Barge Reaearch,
Revised edition ISBN 0-9500515-9-4 in 2002)

This edition ISBN 0-9532422-6-9 by Chaffcutter Books 2003

Printed and bound by Piggott Printers Limited, The Paddocks, Cherry Hinton Road, Cambridge CB1 8DH, England

A Conversation with

Dick, the Dagger

The Life and Times
of Centenarian Bargemaster
Captain Henry Miller BEM

as told to **Tony Farnham**

A transcript of the recording made by Tony Farnham at Dartford, Kent, on 18th January 1975

CHAFFCUTTER

Acknowledgments

My grateful thanks go to Dee and Chris Bristow, Captain Miller's daughter and Son-in-Law; also to Chris Alston, one time sailmaker at Everard's Greenhithe loft; Captain Bob Childs and the late Captain Jim Uglow for their most helpful contributions; Captain Ken Garrett, recently retired Marine Director of F T Everard & Sons for access to and use of his photographic archive; John Reynolds for tug information; Elizabeth and David Wood, Dave Clement, Hugh Perks and Richard Walsh of The Society for Sailing Barge Research for the final editing and typesetting of my draft; and last but not least to my wife Sandra for the onerous task of transcribing the original recordings.

Tony Farnham
Chairman, The Society for Sailing Barge Research
Maidstone
2001

Many of the photographs included in this publication have deteriorated with the passage of time. Some are around 100 years old, and even those more recent are contemporary in the true sense of the word. They are reproduced predominantly without retouching by today's technology, in order to authentically reflect their antiquity.

Contents

Introduction

I grew up in Greenhithe village on the south bank of the London river, into the Sailing Barge community of firms such as Associated Portland Cement Manufacturers and F T Everard and Sons who had their barge and ship repair yard there. Barge repair work was going on in the nineteen-forties, fifties and sixties, but all new building had long since ceased.

On school holidays, most days after school and sometimes days when I should have been in school, I spent on the river, learning to swim, sail and scull large barge boats from an early age. I was also fortunate enough to go away on motor boats and on my friend's father's tug towing lighters (dumb barges) up to the Pool of London and in and out of the docks. The river was very busy in those days (1940's) and I got to know many of the skippers and crews and most of the people associated with the Everard yard. Amongst my acquaintances were shipwrights, blacksmiths, riggers and sailmakers, and I often sat in the sail loft talking and watching Alf Naylor, George Moore and Chris Alston repairing or making new sails for the remaining Everard barges.

I got to know Captain Henry Miller (alias, 'Dick the Dagger') at about that time, and if a young lad showed interest in the barges he would always give you a lot of his time and encouragement. He knew the end of barging was in sight. He retired from the barges at the age of seventy and spent the next ten years as Everard's Gate Keeper, finally retiring at eighty. Whilst he was working at Everards, I spent many an evening in the Gate Keeper's dug-out talking with 'Dick' about the old barging days.

I left school in 1949 at the age of fourteen and went away under sail on the Sailing Barge *Greenhithe* with Captain Bob Roberts, carrying cargoes of cattle cake, cement, peanuts, flour and wheat, etc for the East coast ports. We loaded in the London river overside from ships or from London Docks quays and warehouses, or brought coal from Keadby on the river Trent to Margate or Harwich gas works.

So having done it first hand, so to speak, now looking back I can really relate to what 'Dick' and the other skippers and mates had spoken about when I was growing up. It wasn't until later on that I realised this was a way of life that was soon to be gone forever.

On 11th September 1974, Captain Jim Uglow and I were guests at 'Dick's' 100th birthday party. A telegram had arrived from Her Majesty The Queen and he had also had a visit from the Mayor of Dartford and many other well-wishers. A good celebration was enjoyed by all.

In January 1975 I asked 'Dick's' permission to record an interview with him about his life and times spent under sail all those years ago, relying only on the wind and tide to make a voyage and earn a living. This book includes a transcript of those tapes and it serves also as my tribute to him.

Captain Henry Miller BEM sailed off into the sunset and found his Valhalla at the grand old age of 101 in 1976 and I am proud to have known him. This is his story and it is dedicated to him and all his contemporaries who sailed the London River.

Fair ye well ye last of the Sailorman, you are homeward bound.

Tony Farnham
2001

Preface

This is the story of a man and a way of life that has long faded with the mists of time. Henry Miller was born on 11th September 1874 into mid Victorian Britain.

The Industrial Revolution had begun some many years before and was by then in full and enduring swing. The steam engine had been introduced to sea-going vessels, and large sailing ships, though still carrying cargo to and from far off ports, were soon to find they had to compete with coal fired steamships.

The London Docks were a hive of industry in Dick's day with all manner of vessels coming and going. A dominant feature of the river and coastal scene were the thousands of Thames, Medway and east coast spritsail rigged sailing barges. Picturesque from every angle, whether underway or at anchor, theirs was no idle beauty, for these workhorses carried cargo, fair weather and foul, for generations. They were a cheap means of transport, only relying on a modest crew, wind and tide. The building of these wonderful craft belonged to the age of the adze, the sawpit and the steam chest, and of course the skills of the shipwrights which were then taken for granted, but which would cause wonderment today.

London Watergate (Tower Bridge) was completed in 1894 and Dick had carried cement by sailing barge from Greenhithe up the London River to build the buttresses for the towers. Horse drawn traffic was the norm, hay and straw being brought into the Pool of London by sailing barges, known as Stackies, from east coast farms, returning with stable manure, London mixture as it was known, to fertilize the farmer's fields to complete what was an ecological circle ahead of its time. Dick also recalled the tens of thousands of bricks being transported by barge from the Kentish brickfields to feed the development needs of the world's fastest growing capital city. He also remembered sailing on the Margate 'Hoy' barges to London, collecting the seaside town's weekly shopping needs, with timetable regularity.

He had many people to deal with as he went about his business - dockers, tugmen, lightermen, port officials, customs officers, other bargemen and many more; some diligent, some less so, a colourful variety of characters associated with the comings and goings of that maritime community. He also put his era into context by recalling his reluctance to get stores from Whitechapel when requested to do so by his skipper, a refusal based on fears for his safety midst the spate of murders in the area by the notorious Jack the Ripper.

His was not an easy living; when wind and tide did not serve, or they were weatherbound and unable to collect or deliver their cargoes, they did not get paid. The same applied to times when the Port of London ground to a halt through strikes and other industrial action.

The war years, both WWI and WWII, involved sailing through treacherous minefields, and being subject to enemy air attacks, as happened at Dunkirk in 1940 as he took part in the evacuation of Allied troops from the beaches, rescuing over 200 men by sailing barge, a feat of bravery for which he was awarded the British Empire Medal.

Dick stepped ashore at the age of seventy, taking on the role of gate-keeper at the Everard's Greenhithe yard for a further ten years before finally retiring aged eighty.

Dick, the Dagger was a small wiry man who, despite his years, had a quick and fertile mind and a marvellous ability to recollect many of the events of his past. Sadly, despite a countenance and mobility more akin to a man thirty years younger, Dick passed on to that port of 'Fiddlers Green', and with him has passed the knowledge of a way of life which, though possibly less hurried than that of today, nevertheless had its own urgency - to catch a tide, to gain a cargo, and to earn the most return from what was by any stretch of the imagination a demanding existence.

Over 3,000 sailing barges were built, the majority in Victorian times. At the turn of the 20th century the barge was in its heyday with over 2,000 trading. The vast majority of these were officially registered, but there were also many which traded without ever appearing in the Register. Although new building continued up to the late twenties, the number of barges in commission began to fall away rapidly as the competition of the railways and the increasing payloads of the motor lorry on a rapidly improving road network took their toll. By the end of The Great War around 1,650 still traded; by the time the last new barge was built, only 1,100 plied the coastline; and by the beginning of World War II just 600 still carried cargo. War-time duty without maintenance as barrage balloon moorings and the venerable age of some others which had survived until then, made many beyond economic commissioning after hostilities ended in 1945. Of the 300 or so which did return to peacetime trade, many were soon fitted with auxiliary engines or stripped completely of all their canvas to work as pure motor vessels. As soon as 1950, just 80 remained under sail alone, 40 were auxiliaries and 60 were exclusively under power. Some twenty years on only the *Cambria* carried cargo under sail alone and 1970 was her last year in trade. Most, if not all of the auxiliaries were gone and the motorised barges which survived could be counted on two hands. All have long since been sold out of trade, the last probably the 'ironpot' *Wyvenhoe* which worked on until 1982, just six years short of her centenary.

Of the thousands that were built, around 30 survive in commission as yachts and as passenger charter vessels. But whilst the preservation and ongoing maintenence of this handful of survivors is a noble cause, the difference between sailing one of today's well maintained barges and the existence experienced in a bygone age when Dick worked the tides, is so extreme as to defy comparison.

Tony Farnham

'Dick, the Dagger' Miller with his shipwright father (right), seen aboard one of Dick's barges. Father holds a hammer and brace, his son a hammer, and the windlass has just been fitted with new timber welts.

The Interview

TF   Captain Miller, it's quite an occasion for me to come here today to interview you; you must be the oldest living sailorman. Tell me about yourself, how it all started. When were you born?

D the D   In 1874 on 11th September.

TF   A family of how many?

D the D   Six.

TF   And did your father work on the water?

D the D   No, he was a shipwright for a man called Hugget at Margate.

TF   So you originally came from Margate?

D The D   Yes, I was born in Margate.

TF   At what age did you leave school to work on the water?

D the D   In 1888. I was 13 and went in the *City of London*, a sailing barge owned by Alfred Keep who had the yard at Greenhithe. I was apprentice to them.

TF   How long were you in her?

D the D   *City of London*, well I was in her until she went to the Paris Exhibition[1] in '89. It was a long time ago now. The skipper's son was older than me. I was about 14 then, so he took him instead of me, so I went in the little old stumpie[2], *Avon*.

TF   Was she owned by Keep as well?

D the D   Yes, her skipper at that time was a man called 'Big Ben' Saul.

TF   How many barges did Keep have at that time?

D the D   A tidy few.

---

[1] The World Fair opened in Paris in 1889, its principle landmark being Gustave Eiffel's temporary tower. It was retained initially as a radio mast, but soon became the symbol of Paris and French engineering. Today it remains one of the World's leading tourist attractions.
[2] The Stumpie barge was named for having no topmast, setting a large high peaked mainsail, foresail, mizzen and, in bowsprit Stumpies, a jib.

TF   Do you remember any of their names?

D the D   Yes I do, *City of London, Doffoly, Thames, New York, New Zealand, Baltic, Redwing, Pacific, Atlantic, Adriatic, Minnie, Arctic, Alan, Avon*, plus a few more; can't think of their names.

TF   Where were they trading from?

D the D   Well the bigger ones like *Pacific, Atlantic* and *Adriatic* - another one that I had for several years, London to Margate with coal.

TF   Whereabouts in London were you loading coal?

D the D   Deptford Creek.

TF   So you remember the Deptford Creek road bridge[1], do you?

D the D   Oh yes. We never went up through there, we loaded at the gas works or loaded out of ships.

The 1878 *New York*, built and owned by Alfred Keep, seen discharging into a horse drawn cart at Broadstairs. The ability of sailing barges to take the ground on a foreshore and in drying creeks and harbours allowed loading and unloading overside into carts to be readily undertaken.

---

[1] The Deptford Creek road bridge had a lifting span. It was not unusual for barges to snag their rigging when squeezing through.

TF	When you were running (barges) into Deptford Creek, did you have to use sweeps[1]?
D the D	No, we used to sail them in, we had just enough room to get 'em in.
TF	Now we are here talking about the barges in your life, could you tell me how you got the name 'Dick, the Dagger'?
D the D	All I can tell you is, we was on the yard at Greenhithe. I was in *City of London*. I was only a youngster and the mate of another barge the *Minnie*, Bill Bates, along with his father, and we was a cleaning the spars and he said to me, "Come on 'Dick, the Dagger', let's get on with it." and that name stuck with me ever since.
TF	Can you confirm this? 'Jimmy' Uglow, another old skipper told me you were like a young monkey and could climb any mast or rigging and would slide back down the forestay or wangs and the old skippers on the yard used to say "Look at that young lad, he's as sharp as a dagger".
D the D	Yes, I was always climbing the rigging, sometimes putting new bobs[2] on for other skippers and so on. I was known as 'Dick, the Dagger', the lady tamer, from that day with Bill Bates, but yes, it could also have been at that time as well, I can't be sure[3].
TF	So you worked on the *City of London* trading from London to Margate with coal. How long were you with Keep's?
D the D	Well, I started my apprenticeship at 16 and finished that at 21 and went skipper of the *Thames* when I was 22. That was my first barge as master.
TF	What size was she, Dick?
D the D	We used to take 90 ton of coal to Margate.
TF	Was she a swimmie?[4]
D the D	No, a straight stem barge, topsail rigged, bowsprit and all.
TF	Fast barge, was she?
D the D	Pretty fast.

---

[1] Sweeps are very long oars used to row a barge when there was no wind, or in confined waters if the wind did not serve.
[2] Bob is the bargeman's term for the owner's house flag fixed at the top of the mainmast.
[3] It has been suggested that the barge *City of London* might have carried as her badge the arms of the City of London, the cross of St George with a dagger in the left upper quarter.
[4] Swimmie was the name given to sailing barges with a swim head bow and budget stern, a construction used for the traditional Thames lighters.

TF	Now tell me, it must have been really something in your day coming up Sea Reach. How many barges would be coming up at one time?
D the D	Well, I should think 70 or 80 when the weather's been bad and they have been laid up. It was alive with them, job to get the faster barges passed the slower ones. It was so thick with river traffic.
TF	And this would have been what type of barges?
D the D	Well 'brickies', 'cementies', lime barges.
TF	Any 'stackies' amongst them?
D the D	Yes, all sorts, I have seen 50 or 60 coming out the Medway across the Jenkin's Swatch. We always used the Swatchway if the wind was off the land, we was up to windward, and if the wind was easterly and we was coming up from Margate we would come up outside the Nore then, and of course the Nore lightship was there then. There's a buoy there now.
TF	After you became skipper, what happened then?
D the D	Well I carried on with the job. I had the *Thames* for a couple of years then Keep's had the *Arctic* built for racing.
TF	Was she a wooden barge?
D the D	No; iron barge built at Rennie's at Greenwich and she was a failure, she was built for being lighter than ever, like these skimpless yachts that don't draw the water, only in the middle of them, she drawed to much foreward and they couldn't steer her so they entered her in the race, a complete failure, so she was for sale, but had no takers. After that they sent her back to Rennie's and had two foot put in the foreward of her, dropped her bottom, made her bigger and Harry Wright the Commodore of Keep's firm, he had her, then they built the *Alan* at Battersea and Harry Wright took the *Alan*. Alfred Keep called me in the office one day when I was up there at the yard, 'Dick get your clothes out the *Thames* and take the *Arctic*.' I said 'I don't want her', she was a proper puzzle, she was you know. Anyway I had to take her and I had her until I got tired of her, I asked for a shift - they had a new barge coming out, the *Adriatic*. They said you can have the *Adriatic* if you can get someone to take the *Arctic*. I got the mate of the *Doffoly,* chap we called 'Jippy' to take the *Arctic* and I took this *Adriatic* and I had her for seven years.
TF	And was she a steel barge?
D the D	Yes she was, built on the Humber at Beverly.
TF	And what was she like?
D the D	She was all right; comfortable old barge.

The tiller steered 'Stackie' *Eva Annie* of Maldon sails to windward on the Thames, probably in late Victorian times. The mainsail has reefing points so that the sail can be reduced to clear her stack of hay or straw. One of the crew, usually the mate, stands atop the stack, advising the skipper on the tiller when to wind the barge and keep clear of other craft.

TF	Was she a fast barge?
D the D	Long so middling like, good old sea barge.
TF	Where were you trading on her, Dick?
D the D	Margate, Broadstairs, Ramsgate and thereabouts.
TF	Do you remember the Margate Hoy Company?
D the D	Yes I was in them. I was in the *John Bayly* nine years and *Her Majesty*. I left Keep's when they packed up at Greenhithe and Everard had got the yard then, and he had done the repairs for Keep's. They did a lot of lightering work at Battersea and I could see the firm was going a bit humpty. I had a chance to take this here *John Bayly* being how I was a Margate man and I had her on and off with *Her Majesty* for 9 years running from London to Margate.
TF	With what? What trade?

From a postcard photograph taken around 1900, Margate Harbour with the Margate Hoy Company's barges *John Bayly (?)* and *Her Majesty* alongside the harbour wall, the latter was almost new at the time. Her transom sports her home port carved to starboard, with her Port of Registry, Ramsgate, carved in smaller letters beneath.

Some of the famous 'Shrimp Brand' beers brewed in West Street, Gravesend, Kent. The Russell family purchased the brewery in 1858, expanding the business by the acquisition of breweries at Margate and Ramsgate, as well as one at Writtle, Essex, selling out to Trumans in 1930.

D the D	Oh, shopping goods, general cargo. We used to call at Russell's Brewery, Gravesend for Beer; London Docks, Rankin's Mills for flour and Brunner Monds for Soda; you know, what ever orders the town needed.
TF	What was life like on the barges, Dick, in those days? We are talk ing about some 80 years ago?
D the D	Oh all right, nice comfortable cabins. Bloody hard work, that was the only trouble.
TF	I suppose coming up the London River you had to have your wits about you in those days?
D the D	Yes, we used to have to sail right up to Tower Bridge and sail away again, when I had the *John Bayly*, our wharf was next to Tower Bridge and St Katherine Dock.
TF	Did you use the dock ever?
D the D	No we never went in the dock; only to the wharf.
TF	Did you ever go up into the Upper Pool?
D the D	Oh yes, went up with cement when I was in Everard's firm. We were taking cement to load on ships up there, Dutch, Rotterdam boats.
TF	You once told me about a unique run you did taking cement up river to something special. Can you tell us about that Dick?

This magnificent photograph shows the *John Bayly* alongside Russell's Gravesend Brewery, loaded with beer destined for Margate. She has crates atop her hatches and her side decks are crammed with various sizes of beer barrels. The topsail sheet is out and she awaits the tide to be free of the land. Note what appears to be a house flag above the pole of the mizzen mast.

D the D   What up to Tower Bridge? Yes, well I was only a lad then between 13 and 14, we only did about two cargoes.

TF   And this was from where?

D the D   Johnson's Cement Works above Greenhithe to Tower Bridge[1], or what is now (sic. Tower Bridge). We went to the wharf and they landed the cement on there. This cement was used for building the buttresses for the towers. At about this time Jack the Ripper was about and the skipper gave me a shilling and told me to go over the water into Whitechapel and get some meat and bread. But I was only a kid and frightened with all these murders going on, so I would not go.

---

[1] Tower Bridge was under construction from 1886, being opened in 1894. As the twin bascules spent so much time open to admit vessels bound to and from the Pool of London, the upper walkways were intended to allow pedestrians to continue to cross. After many years closed, they reopened to the public some years ago and are much visited by tourists seeking a novel view of the Thames.

Tower Bridge seen here nearing completion, scaffolding surrounding the top of each tower. Sir Horace Jones was the architect of this Victorian masterpiece, construction under the guidance of Sir John Wolfe Barry. Work began in 1886, the bridge officially opened by HRH The Prince of Wales, later Edward VII, on 30th June 1894. Each lifting bascule weighs over 1,000 tons, hydraulic power first used to raise them; but in recent years, although the hydraulic machinery is preserved and on view, the raising machinery has now been converted to electric power. Tower Bridge, originally known as London Watergate, is the only double bascule lifting bridge to span the Thames.

TF	So you starved that day did you?
D the D	No. I remember the mate went, to my recollection.
TF	So you were three hands on the barges in those days?
D the D	Two on some. We were three on the *City of London* and three on the *Royalty*. Me and my brother Arthur worked the barges ourselves.
TF	Was he ever skipper?
D the D	Yes, one of Payne's barges at Greenhithe. He only had one or two old barges. Can't remember any of the names now.
TF	Where in Greenhithe was Payne situated Dick?
D the D	Why up where the cement works is now, before it was built.
TF	Do you remember Bazley White building barges?
D the D	Yes, at Swanscombe; cement people; called barges names after birds - *Dabchick*, *Cygnet*, *Plover*.
TF	Tell me, Dick, did you ever work up river under bridges?

'Above bridges' meant lowering the barge's gear for the tow up, or if no tow was available or could be afforded, rigging a square 'bridge sail' and working the tides to the berth. Once arrived, the gear all had to be hove up to clear the hatches, so that the cargo could be worked. Here (L-R) the *Elizabeth*, *B & S*, and *Victoria* lie hard by Lambeth Bridge, horse drawn wagons ferrying the freight.

D the D   Yes, I have been right up to Teddington Lock with cement, but we towed up by steam tug so didn't use sweeps or bridge sails then, but have used them. Bloody hard work, bridge work, I can tell you. I can remember the stackies coming into the Pool with fodder for the horses and the barges taking manure away, they were Essex barges - *Veronica* was a stackie. I have seen her deep loaded with hay from Essex ports and *Sirdar* and the *Ready,* later called *Mirosa*. They could also carry cargo under hatches.

TF   Did you ever work a 'stackie' barge?

D the D   No; had nothing to do with them.

TF   What were they like underway?

D the D   Crazy. Sometimes if the wind caught them off guard, sailing a haystack blind at times. They were good seamen, them Essex men. We carried stacks of coke loose only one hatch high, we used to take it into the cement works.

TF   Have you worked any of the rivers or creeks down Swin?

D the D   The Crouch, all them rivers. We run up the Blackwater to Heybridge and Maldon, took coal to Heybridge Basin twice when I had the *Adriatic*.

---

[1] The East Swin or King's Channel is a long established channel in the lower Thames Estuary, giving access to the north.

St Paul's Cathedral is the backdrop for this interesting view c.1910. In the foreground the *May Flower* lies with hatches off, the barge to her right has a stack, much higher over her fore hatch; behind her can be seen a topsail barge devoid of her topmast, presumably making passage as a Stumpie; to the left of the picture a deep laden barge with topmast lowered.

The 'Pool of London' and the
a hive of activity when

At least eight craft lie on the mooring buoy just to port of the barge with a stack well up her mainmast. next to her what looks like a 'Billy-Boy' ketch from the north-east; the Stumpie to the right of the picture is laden, the other barges appear light; the barge with no mast looks to be an old sailing barge hull, much patched, probably in use as a lighter.

A view of Tower Bridge from the south-east taken in the late 1920s, with the twin bascules raised to allow passage of two barges being towed down by a tug. The mule-rigged barge with a white cross on her topsail is one of R & W Paul's craft, the Ipswich millers. The cross device on the topsail represents the sails of a windmill and was used throughout the Paul's fleet.

adjacent parts of the Thames were
'Dick, the Dagger' was barging

The Pool of London photographed c.1890. Ships would berth alongside the riverfront wharves or lie off in the stream being unloaded into lighters of many shapes and sizes. Some were purpose built, some retired sailing vessel hulls, others specialist types from the broad and narrow canal systems. Sailing barges are seen berthed many deep to load for coastwise destinations.

TF   Did you go down to Pin Mill and lpswich?

D the D   Yes, dozens of times when I had the *John Bayly*. We used to go once a month up
            the Orwell to Cranfield's for 88 - 90 tons of flour for Margate and stock it for
            Cranfield at Margate. Then we would sail light for London River on our weekly
            shopping trip picking up goods as we went or the town would miss the week's
            stores.

TF   I expect you have had some bad weather around the coast on some of these trips?

D the D   Yes, pretty bad at times. We laid three weeks in Harwich bound for Yarmouth, about
            a dozen of us, wind easterly all the time.

TF   Could you get ashore?

D the D   Yes we could get ashore for food, thank goodness, but we couldn't get our passage
            down.

TF   Dick, have you ever seen a barge launched where they would build them on the side
            of a river and launch?

A barge launching at the Greenhithe Yard of F T Everard & Sons in 1903. The *Lady Maud* has a bouquet at her stemhead which
traditionally included a sprig of evergreen symbolising longevity. The 'champagne' bottle, also decorated with flowers, is shortly to
be broken on the barge's stem. The shipwrights and others from the yard are gathered aboard and around to witness the occasion.
Presumably nobody has noticed that the Union flag at the bow is upside down. The *Lady Maud* was built for Charles Charleton for
the cement trade, but was bought back by F T Everard in 1915.

20

D the D	Yes, I witnessed the *Cambria* and *Hibernia*.
TF	Were they being launched on the same day?
D the D	Yes, they were.
TF	I believe it was quite an occasion for these small yards on day of a launching?
D the D	Yes it was a good old booze up.
TF	Now what happened when they launched the barge, Dick?
D the D	They would build a slip so they would slide down into the water.
TF	I have seen photos of barges being launched sideways, have you seen any like this?
D the D	No, but they used to launch barges like this around Faversham and Sittingbourne, not enough width there to launch them stern first into the creeks.

Cambria leaving Margate in 1957, by which time she was one of very few barges surviving under sail alone. The topsail, foresail and mainsail are set and the crew are at the windlass raising the anchor.

Hibernia awaits the tide and her tug for the passage down the River Trent from her berth. There was often insufficient water to lie alongside so the cargo was carried across precarious planks to and from the quay.

TF	How long did they take to build a barge in those days?
D the D	Well, it all depends if a damaged barge came for repair, they would take the men off to put her right first. They would build a barge in about three months. Not big barges like *Hibernia*. They took five months to build them. They had a good lot of shipwrights, Most of Everard's came from Yarmouth, Fellows yard.

The Thames during the 'big freeze' of 1895, with the tiller steered topsail barge *Esther* of Maldon on the inside berth.

A lively breeze off Greenwich in 1892. Sailing barges and other craft lie anchored off the windward shore whilst the two barges, barge boats towing astern, carry the tide on a broad reach. Both have brailled their mizzen and some cloths off the mainsail, the following barge also having 'rucked' her topsail.

TF	Tell me Dick, when did you join Everard's; after the Margate Hoy Company?
D the D	Yes, Everard bought the two barges *John Bayly* and *Her Majesty* so they bought the barges and me as well. I took *Her Majesty* when they bought them. I brought the *John Bayly* to Greenhithe first, then Mr Everard, the old man, said 'Now go to Grays and get *Her Majesty*.' as a Grays skipper who lived there would not bring her over. So over I went and sailed her to Greenhithe yard. Mr Everard said 'Now you're back again, hope you're going to stop' and I did. I took *Her Majesty*. I did one trip to Antwerp, carried pitch.
TF	What year would that have been, Dick?
D the D	Just after the First World War; 1919.

A company owned portrait of founder Frederick T Eberhardt, who changed both his and the company name to Everard in 1917.

TF	What was it like going across the channel in the barge, Dick?
D the D	All right if the weather was all right, all wrong if it wasn't.
TF	Would this have been daylight sailing, or night as well?
D the D	Day and night, we carried on.
TF	I expect you got to know the Channel pretty well?
D the D	I didn't know much about it at first but I was a quick learner.
TF	Did you navigate by charts?
D the D	Oh yes, and compass.
TF	How long was an average trip across the Channel by sailing barge?
D the D	Of course it depended where you was going. I come over from Calais to Sandwich in four and a half hours and I went from North Foreland to Dunkirk in just over four hours. We were empty when I had the *Scot*.

The Kent River Stour at Sandwich c.1896. To the left can be seen W Felton's saw mills and shipyard, with the sailing barge *Trilby* in frame. The *Winifred* lies in the middle of the channel at low water, a plank providing access from the quayside; she was built at Felton in 1893 and owned by The Sandwich Hoy Company. By 1920 she was registered at Colchester, Essex and owned by The London & Rochester Barge Company.

TF   You had the *Scot*, the same one that 'Knocker' Hart had in later years?

D the D   Yes that's right.

TF   Now, can you tell me, after you joined Everard's and took *Her Majesty,* what happened then?

D the D   Well, as I said, I did that one trip to Antwerp, then I came back and Captain Harry Layzell of *Marguerite,* he was with us on that trip and he wouldn't go no more, so I turned over out of the (sic. *Her*) *Majesty* to the *Marguerite*.

TF   Can you tell us about the *Marguerite*?

D the D   Well, she was a Swedish built barge sailed over with timber; re-rigged into London River style barge. There were three Swedish built barges, the *Lina, Spencer* and *Marguerite*. Everard didn't go to Sweden to have these built you know. They were built and sailed over with timber on the off-chance of being sold. Everard didn't buy them new; they came from someone at Grays, anyhow.

TF   Were they like normal Thames Spritsail Barges or different?

D the D   No. They were caulk-sided and changed to sprit rig from gaff rig when they came here.

TF	Dick, what was the *Marguerite* like?
D the D	Good barge when I first had her.
TF	Was she a big barge?
D the D	Fifty ton.
TF	How long did you have her?
D the D	I had her three different times; *Marguerite* to *Scot*, *Lady Mary*, back into *Marguerite*.
TF	All this time you were working on the Everard barges, I believe they were still building[1] at the Greenhithe yard?
D the D	Yes, he built a lot of barges.

The 1901 Swedish built *Marguerite* sprit rigged as a staysail barge subsequent to conversion from gaff rig as built. This photograph was probably taken following time on the yard for a refit as her sides are immaculate, devoid of the scars and salt stains which a few months in trade would bestow. Note that in addition to her bob (flag) on the topmast, she is flying a pennant from the mizzen sprit and a flag atop the mizzen mast.

[1] Frederick T Everard was yard manager at Keep's Greenhithe barge yard when in 1880 he acquired the yard, building and repairing sailing barges. Concurrently he became a barge owner, reputedly in settlement of a debt to the yard. The first barge built from scratch at the yard for Everard operation was the *Lord Kitchener* in 1899; the last, the *Cambria* and *Hibernia*, just six years later, though barge repairs continued at Greenhithe until the mid-sixties when the *Will Everard* was sold. (Source: Everard of Greenhithe, K S Garrett, World Ship Society 1991)

TF   Could you remember some of the names?

D the D   The *Lord Kitchener*, *Britisher*, *Anglo-American*, *Scotia*, *Doffoly*, *Cambria*, *Hibernia*, *Briton*, *Scot*, *Lady Mary*, *Lady Maud*, *Grit I*, she was a wooden auxilIary ketch, a War loss. They built another, *Grit II* and *Heron* for Bevan's at Northfleet.

The Everard built *Lady Mary* was launched in 1900 from the Greenhithe yard for Charles Charleton of Greenhithe. She was purchased by Everard in 1915 and saw service in their ownership through two World Wars, ending her days as a mast store moored alongside the Thames saltings at Erith for the Erith Yacht Club. Her own mast and rigging saw further service in the *Kathleen* when she was re-rigged as a yacht in the mid-sixties. Her Davey & Co[1] stem blocks have survived *Kathleen's* demise and are now in use aboard the steel sailing barge *Wyvenhoe*, a product of Forrestt's Wivenhoe yard in 1898.

TF   In those early days, what was the average hours a man worked ashore in the shipyards?

D the D   From 6 am to 5 pm.

TF   And what about wages in those days?

---

[1] Davey & Co started life at Leadenhall Street in February 1885, soon moving to 88 West India Dock Road, London, where it traded for almost a century before moving to nearby Grenade Street, and then to Essex in 1988. Still in business as 'Ships Chandlers' and making many items that have been in production throughout much of the last century, they are a unique source for otherwise unobtainable maritime fittings, though it is acknowledged that these days many of their wares are bound for pub bars rather than sailing ships.

D the D	(Chuckling) What they got, not a lot!
TF	Well can you tell us what you got?
D the D	As I said, not a lot. After the cement works opened up at Greenhithe, we had the contract to carry the clay for the cement works. and we used to work all hours, day and night.
TF	Were you paid by the freight?
D the D	Yes.
TF	How much would you have got for a freight of clay?
D the D	I used to draw £9.00 a week. That was between me (Skipper) and my mate. He had £3.00 and I had £6.00. This was when the Kent Cement Works first opened, can't tell you the year. We did this for three years carrying clay. It was a dirty job and a hard job, the hardest job I ever had in my life.

The Chapman Lighthouse constructed on stilts in the Thames estuary to mark the Chapman Sand off Canvey Island, Essex. Although this lighthouse is no longer in place, the abandoned structure of a similar light can be seen marking the seaward side of the Gunfleet Sand off Clacton, Essex.

TF	Did you load the barge yourself?
D the D	No, we had job enough sailing them. Every night we was in Sea Reach then, up or down.
TF	Where were you picking the clay up from?
D the D	Why, opposite Chapman Head Light, on this side (Kent).
TF	This was a mud hole[1]?
D the D	Yes.
TF	Can you tell me about the people who loaded the barges, the 'Muddies'?
D the D	We had a steam crane at that mud hole, at some of the others gangs of men, often families; grandfathers, fathers, sons, all worked as 'Muddies' loading barges every tide. Bloody hard dirty work it was, I can tell you.

[1] The manufacture of cement involved the use of clay or mud as a flux to bind the mix of chalk during the firing process at the cement works. Much of the clay was carried by old sailing barges from the 'mud holes' in the Thames and Medway estuaries, where the saltings yielded rich blue-grey clay, with few impurities. 'Muddies' was the name given to a tough breed of men who dug the clay from the saltings and loaded it into a barge's hold. This was arduous work, carried on regardless of weather conditions, frequently in places remote from shelter and 'civilisation', the Muddies sometimes living in damp condition aboard hulks close by the mud holes. The job required both strength and skill, for each piece of clay weighed 28 lbs on the 18" x 5" blade of the wooden 'Fly' shovel, cut and thrown up to 25 feet into the barge's hold in a single action. (Source: Cement, Mud & 'Muddies', F G Willmott, Meresborough Books 1977)

The Royal Terrace Pier at Gravesend was built at a time of 'Pier Fever' as a result of the development of pleasure steamer traffic. A temporary pier was built at nearby Northfleet, which was so successful that steamer trade to the Town Quay at Gravesend, where passengers were ferried ashore by watermen, was undermined. A temporary pier was built on the Town Quay but just before completion was smashed up in a riot by watermen who feared for their livelihood. When the permanent Town Pier was opened in 1834 it was so extravagantly constructed that it incurred large debts for Gravesend Corporation. In 1835 the Blockhouse Fort site was purchased by some local councillors who immediately erected a temporary pier called the Terrace Pier. The Municipal Reform Act of 1834 caused the demise of Gravesend Corporation as Town Pier proprietors and the new owners, the Borough Council, took the Terrace Pier owners to court, a battle over pier rights which went on until 1842 and left both parties financially exhausted. During this time a new permanent pier was built at Rosherville, to serve the Gardens at Northfleet and another short lived temporary pier at Marine Parade to the western end of Gravesend. In 1842 a contract was signed for the temporary Terrace Pier to be rebuilt then sold with the adjacent gardens to the Borough Council, when complete, for the sum of £42,000. The Pier was erected but, following a series of evasive legal manoeuvres, was never sold to the Borough. Competition between the Piers had forced tolls down to uneconomic levels, and the coming of the railway in 1849 was the final straw, leaving both piers and their operators bankrupt. At the Town Pier some bondholders who had helped finance the original building had a bailiff seize the Borough regalia including the mace and Aldermen's robes! Eventually the Town Pier was sold to the Tilbury & Southend Railway in 1884 and in 1885 the Royal Terrace Pier was sold to a company belonging to the local pilots which it still serves to this day. The Town Pier has now received a multi-million pound grant from the European Community to fund its restoration. (Principle source: A History of Gravesend, R H Hiscock, Phillimore 1976)

Greenwich Pier in 1906 with a dozen barges in view. In the near background can be seen a Swimmie barge and a laden Stackie at anchor.

TF	It's quite something, you know Dick, sitting here with you talking. You're over 100 years old now and can still remember so much about your life. Man has learnt to fly and has landed on the moon in your lifetime and no doubt you can remember the streets of London when there were just horses. Can you remember the first cars?
D the D	Yes, I can remember as if it was yesterday.
TF	What were the London streets like then?
D the D	Not so busy as now; lots more people walking; but we didn't get up into the streets of London a lot. We only went to Deptford to load coal. We used to go straight in. The ship would come in, we would load and out we would come. We didn't very often get off and up to London unless we was in the docks, Poplar and around about there; Limehouse.
TF	I believe there was quite a lot of unemployment in those days?
D the D	Yes there was.
TF	And were people encouraged to go on the barges?
D th D	It was no problem to get a crew, it was not too bad pay, food was cheap.
TF	What was the price of a loaf of bread or a piece of meat?
D the D	You could buy beef, fourpence a pound, loaf of bread thruppence, pint of beer tuppence. The good old days; go ashore with a shilling you was landed! We were quite well off compared with some people. When we started going over on the continent we earned more money.
TF	I want to talk to you about your trips. Where did you go to, Dick?
D the D	I have been to Antwerp, Nieuport, Rotterdam, Treport, Ostend, Dieppe, Calais, Boulogne, Caen, Fécamp.
TF	Was this after the first World War, and what cargoes were you carrying?
D the D	Yes, Pitch and coal, pitch for road making.
TF	Where did you take the pitch from?
D the D	Beckton Gas Works or East Greenwich. This pitch came from the coke. Then we run a lot of coal when I had the *Scot* from Sandwich to Calais, coal from the Kent coal fields.
TF	You were trading right through the years after the First World War, up to prior the Second World War 1939, what barges did you have?
D the D	Mostly *John Bayly* then.

The year before the Second World War on the Everard yard at Greenhithe. The Training Ship *Worcester* forms the backdrop, the clipper *Cutty Sark* has yet to arrive. The *Sara* and *Veronica* are being prepared for the 1938 Thames Barge Match, though it was not to be their year as *Veronica*, which led the fleet at both start and finish, was disqualified for setting too many headsails, and *Sara* managed only fourth in the Champion Bowsprits, far below expectations. It was not all bad news for Everards, for their home-built *Cambria* won the Coasting Class with the giant *Will Everard* in third place. It was to be another 15 years before the championship of the London River was contested again, and by then the days of the commercial sailing barge were all but finished.

R & W Paul's *Barbara Jean*, built in 1924, seen here in July 1937. After the Goldsmith and Everard giant steel barges, Paul's *Barbara Jean* and sister ship *Aidie* were the largest sailing barges built, Mule rigged and sporting wheelhouses, they were both destined to be war victims.

TF Now, when war was declared Dick, you carried on working on the barge?

D the D Yes, but we were not allowed to sail at night time, not unless they didn't catch us, we used to, we had to, to get our passage. The navy patrols were on the look out, but they did not very often pick you up. Picked me up once, told me not to do it again.

TF Now I know you went to Dunkirk in June 1940. How did that come about?

D the D Well we was at Greenhithe, I had the *Royalty* then laying off awaiting orders. Mr Everard called me ashore and told me they were going to take us to Ramsgate. We thought we were going to unload a ship sunk on the Goodwins and we were going to lighten her. Anyhow, the tug came for us; one of Alexander's Sun tugs from Gravesend, took us to Southend that night. Next day we towed to Ramsgate with the *Tollesbury* and then went to Dover; laid in there two or three days. There was a lot of barges in there, they was all loading cargoes.

TF Can you name any of them?

D the D Yes I can. *Ethel Everard*, (and) *Aidie*, *Barbara Jean*, both Pauls of lpswich, they were loading. We were one of the last to load. They then told us the tug *Cervia* would be taking us out the dock, destination unknown; Captain of the tug would

The tug *Cervia* in an earlier guise as the *Tamesa* when in the ownership of the United Steam Tug Co. She became *Cervia* when taken over by William Watkins Limited and is seen here off Gravesend, her base under both owners.

have your orders. We had a rough guess when we was loaded, where we was going. So they towed us all across the channel towards Dunkirk. We were told to put the barges ashore and the soldiers would unload us.

TF   What was your cargo, Dick?

D the D   Food, cans of water and ammunition.

TF   So you had live ammunition, did you?

D the D   Yes, live shells and all the cargo was below hatches, none on deck.

TF   What was it like when you arrived off Dunkirk, had it already started then?

D the D   Yes they (The German Army and Luftwaffe) had already started firing and shelling right along the sand. All the soldiers had gone off the sand and gone out onto the jetty, we put *Royalty* ashore and only half an hour later a French officer come in a pinnace and told us 'Get out of her, we are going to blow her up'.

TF   How many barges were there at the time?

D the D   Lots; all them others were ashore. The tide was coming in and I had put her (*Royalty*) ashore where I could. Soon as he told us to get out of her, we got in the boat and rowed off to the tug. He was awaiting for us out there. All the other crews had gone off the barges. We were not near them, couple of mile up the beach at Malo Les Bains.

Dick, the Dagger's barge *Royalty*, her boat towing astern, makes her way deep laden down the dock to lock out into the Thames on 26th July 1939, just a couple of months before war was declared.

TF   Who was in the boat with you?

D the D   The mate (Kenny Coe), my son, Ernie, who was third hand and some soldiers who
          had come aboard at Dover. They was to help unload, so we was all in the barge boat
          rowing out to the tug when there come a Jerry plane, dropped a couple of bombs,
          missed, then come back and machine gunned us. Missed again. It was a bit hot I can
          tell you. They bombed and sunk two destroyers while we was there, direct hits. We
          got out to the tug and the skipper said we can not do any good here, so we come
          back down and then saw the barge *Tollesbury* at anchor. We went alongside. I got on
          the barge and found about 150 soldiers down in her hold. There was no wind so she
          was not going anywhere, so we passed her tow rope over to the tug. We broke the
          windlass getting the anchor free, then we started towing to Ramsgate. During our
          trip back we picked up a lifeboat from the Orient Liner *Orion* loaded with about 25
          soldiers. Some had been shot up pretty badly, the boat's engine had broken-down
          and no-one knew how to fix it.

R & W Paul's sailing barge *Tollesbury* escaped from the Dunkirk beaches packed with soldiers, some badly wounded. Capt Miller's
recollection of around 150 was understated, as including those picked up from the *Orion's* lifeboat, she had some 270 soldiers aboard for
the tow back to England by the *Cervia*. Following disembarkation of the returning troops at Ramsgate she was refitted for further service.
She was recently rebuilt at Ipswich and has now spent some years as a wine bar in London's Docklands.

TF   Pretty harrowing time by the sound of it, Dick, on the beaches at Dunkirk?

D the D   Yes it was, but luckily we didn't have a lot of it.

TF   What happened when you arrived back to Ramsgate?

D the D   Well, we put the soldiers ashore and then the tug towed the *Tollesbury* to Gravesend.

TF   They didn't ask you to go back to Dunkirk for another trip?

The *Ethel Everard* languishes on the beach at Dunkirk shortly after the last of the troops to successfully flee the advancing German Army had left for England. Some days later, *Ethel Everard's* sails already in tatters, the photograph reproduced below was taken for use by the German High Command propaganda machine - "Soldiers of the West front! Dunkirk has fallen ... with it has ended the greatest battle in world history. Soldiers, my confidence in you knew no bounds. You have not disappointed me." wrote Adolf Hitler on 5th June 1940.

D the D	No, by the time we was back at Gravesend they was almost all out of Dunkirk. It would have been too late then.

A 1940 photo showing R & W Paul's sailing barge *Aidie* abandoned on Dunkirk beach, with the *Lark* beached in the breakers behind. The foreshore was littered with vehicles of all kinds, many of which had been commandeered by the retreating troops, and which on arrival were arranged to provide some makeshift cover from the Axis gunfire.

TF	Now, for going on this harrowing voyage at the age of 65 years, you were shortly afterwards invested by King George VI at Buckingham Palace.
D the D	Us bargemen all volunteered to go over you know. When they got us together at Dover, we didn't know where we were going exactly, and some of the poor devils never came back. Mr Everard told me I had to go to the Palace and get the B.E.M on so and so day. So me and my son went up, shook hands with the King, (we) had a chat about Dunkirk, pinned on my medal and said 'Well done skipper'.
TF	You are one of about five sailormen to get awards during the World War II for bravery while working on the barges. Tommy Willis and Jimmy Uglow got the M.B.E and a couple of other East Coast skippers got the B.E.M, but there aren't many of you, Dick. After your investiture by the King, what happened then?
D the D	Well, I carried on barging right through the war.
TF	Did you have more rough times?
D the D	We were stopped several times and had some uncomfortable nights, specially when they stopped you soon as it got dark and made you anchor. The Navy didn't have much idea where a barge could or couldn't anchor, so we had many rough nights rollin' our guts out.
TF	Were you restricted where you could go on the barges during war time?
D the D	You got your sailing instructions from Southend first, then the Downs if you were bound across the Channel. Some of the barges were lost during the war striking mines, Everard's *Britisher* was one of these.
TF	Did you ever come through any minefields?

36

D the D   Yes, I have been through them several times.

TF   Did you know they were there?

D the D   Only as they told us. We come from Antwerp and we come down the coast to Calais.
            Our sailing instructions was from there to the South Foreland and the Downs, but we
            got to Dunkirk and the wind dropped and the tide was against us, so we had to
            anchor. Well just at dark that night the tide become right for us to get a start; there
            comes a nice breeze off the land and the other barges that was with us, they carried
            on down towards Calais from Dunkirk, that's twenty miles. Well me and my
            brother um'd and ah'd and we made up our minds we was going to chance it across,
            so we went over from Dunkirk to the North Foreland, not the South Foreland. We
            got across just at daylight, just nice and clear, when we looked around there's
            another of our barges must have followed us over, right through the minefields, in
            the dark. It was the little *Marguerite* and I had *Her Majesty* then.

            Another time I went through the minefields, we had orders from the Downs to carry
            on to Dunkirk, Calais or Boulogne. And we got half channel over, and the wind
            dropped, and the tide set us through the minefields. We couldn't help ourselves, we
            couldn't do nothing about it.

TF   This was World War I, Dick, was it? Could you see the mines?

D the D   We just got a glimpse now and again in the sea. They was well down about ten feet.
            We was drawing six feet.

This photograph is of the harbour at Dieppe at the end of the First World War. Thames Sailing Barges, around forty of them, which have been
supplying the advancing British troops with stores and ammunition are dressed overall to celebrate victory in the 'War to end Wars.'

TF	You were a wooden barge so if you had touched one would you have gone up?
D the D	Gone up I expect. Touch one of the buttons on the mine, you couldn't help it, it was all down to the tide setting us in amongst them.
TF	The times you were sailing during the World War II, were you ever attacked by planes?
D the D	No, only attacked at Dunkirk, we were machine gunned then, shelled and bombed as we went along. We was lucky I suppose. I was worried about these here planes machine gunning us and the bullets going through the hatches and hitting the shells stacked in the hold. This was all happening as I was putting her ashore, but we soon got out or her as I told you.
TF	Now after the war finished, did you still continue on the barges?
D the D	Yes I kept on until I was seventy. Then spent ten years as gatekeeper on the Everard yard at Greenhithe; thought I better retire at eighty and make room for a few of the youngsters who were coming up to their 65th birthday. They might like the job as gate keeper.

The Everard sail loft at Greenhithe was a hive of activity, especially after severe weather when repairs would be the priority, or in the weeks leading up to the Barge Matches, when new sails would be made and old ones recut to gain that extra knot. Chris Alston and Arthur 'Benny' Bennett apply their skills, Benny sewing the bolt rope to a barge's foresail.

TF	You have said you carried on after the war. What barge did you have then?
D the D	I took the *Marguerite*. It was my third time in her and I carried on until we had to go ashore to have a new stem in, and with a gale of wind blowing one night, she broke adrift and smashed herself up. So they done away with her, broke her up and burnt her at Greenhithe.
TF	Now, can you tell me something about the early barge matches, Dick. Did you ever take part in any of the races yourself?
D the D	I was in the *Cambria* two or three races, *Alf Everard*. In the *Britannia* when she belonged to Stone's at Northfleet.
TF	How many barges used to take part in those early days?
D the D	Tidy few at times.
TF	You used to start from where?
D the D	We started in Gravesend Reach, start off the Ship and Lobster pub.
TF	Do you remember some of the famous early barges in the races?
D the D	*Giralda*, *Haughty Belle*, she was built aft like a yacht, round stern. *Daisy Little*, she won the race one year. *Plinlimmon*, *Fortis*. *Harold Margetts*, *Ethel Margetts*, they both belonged to cement people up under Medway Bridge. The races used to finish at Erith, start Gravesend, down around the Mouse Light and back to Erith. Later they all finished races at Gravesend. Everard had several champions over the years; *Princess*,

The steel built *Fortis* from J H Fellows' yard at Great Yarmouth in 1898. It is hard to imagine that she was just a third of the gross tonnage of the 'Big Four' Everard barges from the same yard less than thirty years later.

Above, *Haughty Belle*, with her rounded forefoot and counter looking more like a racing yacht than a sailing barge, to the extent that other barge owners claimed that she should not be allowed to compete in the matches. She was certainly very out of the ordinary, all the more surprising as her owners, for whom she was built in 1896, were E J & W Goldsmith, a firm unique in building sailing barges to standard designs with interchangeable sails and rigs. Below, the much more conventional *Daisy Little* shared with *Haughty Belle* the distinction of winning a match in her year of build; for the *Daisy Little* the 1891 Medway Match, the winner's pennant presented by C H Curel who had built her shortly before the race; for the *Haughty Belle* the Thames Match. Overall there was nothing to choose between their racing records, and both returned to racing when almost 40 years old, still competitive amongst the large turn-outs of the late Twenties and early Thirties.

Veronica and *Sara*. She was champion in my young day, faster than *Giralda*. Held the course record for years, a lovely little barge she was.

TF   Did you get in any escapades with the Customs in early days bringing anything over?

D the D   Got caught at Sandwich once. I only had one bottle; they took it away from me!

TF   You did tell me another little tale once. What was that?

D the D   Oh yes, he was a cocky bloke. I was on the jetty pier at Margate one Sunday morning. We wasn't loaded, I had come home by train and I was talking to young Teddy Parker what was Coxswain of the lifeboat. He used to do the pilots, land the pilots and I was a telling him I got two freights to Margate and two to Ramsgate, bricks from Ostend. So this here joker, he was close to me and said, '...and don't you bring anything over or I'll have you'. I said 'All right, we ain't gone yet'. Anyhow, we come from Ostend and we come into the Foreland and it's just getting dark, so I said to my mate, 'Don't put any lights up'. We come up along the land and anchored off the jetty in the dark. My brother 'Dusty' and them was in this here Pilot Boat. I rowed ashore in the boat and called them. They were waiting for us and I said I got some stuff aboard, so they came and got it and took it ashore. When the tide comes for us to go in the harbour, we went in and turned in. We are all turned in, when down he comes, but he was (too) late, (chuckling) that's all there was to it. We had already unshipped it, it was gone, we done the same again at Ramsgate.

TF   Was there quite a lot of this going on in those days?

D the D   Yes, and a lot got caught as well.

TF   Dick, can you tell me about the sailing ships in your days, you must have seen some of the famous ones?

D the D   I have been aboard of that one (pointing up to a painting on the wall). The *Thermopylae* and I have been aboard the *Cutty Sark* when they laid in the West India Dock. We loaded cask cement into them for Australia, they bought wool home and took cargoes of cement back out.

TF   So you can remember the sailing ships coming up the London River and also in the Channel?

D the D   I can recollect one of those ships, don't know what one it was. I was in the barge *Whitwell*, bound for Rye with timber and we was getting well down towards Dungeness. About 5 mile off Dungeness we see one of these ships a coming under sail and you know that ship caught us before we got round Dungeness, full rigged ship she was, under all sail she was a travelling.

TF   So you can tell me about the *Cutty Sark* can you?

The Watkins' tug *Muria* towing the renowned Tea Clipper, *Cutty Sark* up the Thames to Greenhithe from Falmouth on 18th June 1936. Prior to her arrival she was owned by a Captain Dowman until his death, following which his widow presented her to the Thames Nautical Training College. After twent-five years she was handed over to the Cutty Sark Preservation Society and was placed in the dry dock at Greenwich in 1954, where she has been open to the public for almost fifty years.

D the D	Yes, I went aboard the *Cutty Sark* when the tug *Muria* brought her up the Thames in 1936 for the last time. I was aboard the *Cambria* and we took the *Worcester* training ship cadets down Sea Reach and put them aboard the *Cutty Sark* and they towed her up and she laid outside the *Worcester* at Greenhithe.
TF	You can remember the sailing ships in the London Docks, it must have been a hive of industry in those days?
D the D	Yes, all the docks had jetties then, before they made them into wharves, so each sailing ship or steamer laid to a jetty.
TF	Could you tell me about the 'Bawley' boats that used to fish for shrimps and whitebait off Gravesend? What was the Thames like in those days; was it cleaner?
D the D	Cleaner? Yes a lot cleaner. I recollect old 'Youngy', he had the little Bawley named the *Liberty*. He used to stand for shrimps at Greenhithe and catch them.
TF	What was the water like there and up river?
D the D	Cleaner. I've drinked the water at Waterloo Bridge, it was that good.
TF	And you can remember the Leigh Bawlies and no doubt the sailing fishing drifters and trawlers?

D the D	Well, out of Great Yarmouth I have seen as many as eighty sail, Scottish and Yarmouth vessels, all herrings, miles of herrings!
TF	How much?
D the D	Oh, you used to go alongside with a bucket and they would fill it for you, they used to give them to you.
TF	Was there much rivalry in those days between the Sailorman and Fisherman?
D the D	There was no rivalry like that, but only rivalry to get a berth and to unload their fish. They all had to go into the market. There was rivalry between sailormen to get a berth first so you could get a cargo, make a decent passage, before the weather come bad on you and you might be stuck there for days, wind or weather bound. If you didn't get your passage, well, you didn't get paid, that's what it was all about.
TF	What's your impression of things today, Dick; the barging world today that you know and read about?
D the D	Well it's finished; there's no bargemen now properly, they're yachtsmen now.
TF	What do you think of the likes of us that are trying to keep barges alive?
D the D	I think its a good thing, but I don't believe these here yachtsmen are as good or have the touches a bargeman himself had. We was always a shifting something, slack the mast back or pull it up a bit higher; trim the sails so we could make 'em go a bit better.
TF	These barges, Dick, are part of our national maritime heritage, so we have got to try to keep it all going.
D the D	But they won't last for ever will they?
TF	No, we know that, most of them are already 70, 80 or 90 years old now, but it's surprising that in recent years and especially in the last two or three years, more and more barges are being re-rigged than ever.
D the D	Well some of the barges were built of Oak and they have lasted well, the old *Cambria* she's been practically re-built or re-sheathed, they could do that with a lot of the barges now. These here yacht barges, they could sheath them, and they would last another twenty years.
TF	Well, Dick, time's getting on and I would like to thank you very much for this fascinating talk. You have such a wonderful memory and I think you are a wonderful old man and a real credit to all the sailormen who have ever sailed out of the London River.

Postscript

Captain Henry Miller, together with other Everard personnel who had played a part, was invited back to the Dunkirk Beaches in 1950, the 10th Anniversary of those harrowing and unimaginable days of war. They were carried across aboard F T Everard & Sons' Motor Vessel *Alacrity*. No doubt, as Henry Miller relived the nightmare of those dreadful days, he spared a thought for his Mate, Kenny Coe, a young Greenhithe man, who had left Everard's sailing barges after that fateful trip. He had joined one of the firm's motor ships, the *Adaptity*. He was to lose his life not long after when, on the 5th October 1940, his ship struck a mine off Harwich in position 51°44N, 01°17E, whilst on passage from London to Grimsby with ground nuts.

The Mayor and Mayoress of Dartford present Captain Henry 'Dick, the Dagger' Miller with Her Majesty the Queen's congratulatory telegram on 11th September 1974, his 100th birthday.

Tony Farnham (left) looks on as Captain Jim Uglow MBE, a mere 70 year old, shows centenarian Captain Miller his book 'Sailorman, a Barge Master's Story' which had recently been published at the time.

On 11th September 1975 Captain Henry Miller celebrated his 101st birthday. That November he received a letter from The Company of Watermen and Lightermen congratulating him on his age and confirming that he was the oldest living Freeman of The Waterman's Company of the River Thames.

On 2nd January 1976 Captain Henry 'Dick, the Dagger' Miller passed away, aged 101, at his home in Dartford, Kent.

Appendix I

Reproduction of the original Deposition on oath by Henry Miller covering the loss of the *Royalty*, dated 10th June 1940.

Inq. 1.

EXAMINATION ON OATH.

IN PURSUANCE OF THE 465TH SECTION OF THE MERCHANT SHIPPING ACT, 1894, 57 AND 58 VICTORIÆ,
CAP 60.

ISSUED BY THE
BOARD OF TRADE.

Henry James Miller of 2 Carlton Gdns London Rd Greenhithe .... being duly sworn,

deposes as follows ; namely,

1. That he, being the holder of a ~~certificate of~~ watermans licence , numbered 33456 was ~~is~~ Master of the sailing ~~ship~~ barge Royalty of the port of Rochester of the ~~gross~~ net registered tonnage of 85 tons, her official number being 109919 ; that the ship was built of wood . at Rochester in the year 1895 , that she was classed by Lloyds as A.1 , that her engines were of ~~horse power~~ and that she was rigged as a spit sail barge .

2. That the ship was ~~is~~ owned by F.T.Everard & Sons Ltd of the Wharf, Greenhithe in the County of Kent . ~~and was under charter to Government .~~

3. That the ship carried a crew of 3 hands including deponent, and six soldiers ~~passengers~~. ~~The name of the pilot was~~

4. That the ship had on board a cargo of Army stores of the weight of about 50 tons shipped by the Admiralty ~~at Dover~~ and consigned to the Flanders Army ~~or and that tons of were carried on deck.~~

5. That the ship sailed from Dover being towed on her intended voyage to Malo les Bains in France on the 31st day of May 1940 , at 10 p.m.; that the draught of water of the said ship at the time of sailing was 3 feet 6 inches forward and 5 feet 6 inches aft.

6. That at the time of sailing as above the said ship was well found in every respect, having full regulation life saving appliances.

7. That the said ship was proceeding on the intended voyage as above stated & reached Malo les Bains where she was under orders to beach the craft, discharge cargo

(5271) 4000 Wt.5405/305 7000 12/35 T.B.H.K. Gp.512 Ltd.

with the help of soldiers in occupation & to embark soldiers for return journey. When "Royalty" arrived at Malo les Bains at about 7. A.M. 1st June, soldiers were already on the march to Dunkirk.

[Continued on page 4 if necessary].

8. That on Saturday the 1st day of June 1940, at 8 A.m., the weather being fine the wind blowing at force 2 from the W.S.W. the tide being 2 hrs to High water with a slight swell from the seaward the said ship was breached.

The Master, crew & six soldiers got away in the ships life boat, & though severely bombed & machine gunned from the air reached the tug without casualties. The tug returned to Ramsgate picking up on the way & taking in tow a motor launch with about 25 soldiers & also the barge "Tolsbury" with about 200 aboard.

[Continued on page 4 if necessary].

9. That services to the said ship were rendered as follows : *nil* .

[Continued on page 4 if necessary]

10. That in consequence of the aforementioned casualty *no* lives were lost : that the lives of the master *a* crew and *six ~~soldiers~~* ~~passengers~~ (*9* in all) were saved by *Watkins Tug* , the survivors subsisting on board that vessel from *about 8.30 AM to 7.0 PM. 1/6/40* when ~~they~~ were landed at *Ramsgate &* *~~soldiers~~* *be crew continued journey to Gravesend which was reached*

11. That the loss ~~on the said ship is estimated by~~ *at about 10 am. 2/6/* pounds sterling, and on the said cargo at ~~pounds sterling, and that the ship~~ ~~was insured in the sum of~~ pounds sterling, the cargo in pounds ~~sterling, and the freight in~~ ~~pounds sterling.~~

12. That in deponent's opinion the cause of the casualty was *as stated* .

~~and that it might have been avoided~~

13. That the above statements are correct and true to the best of deponent's knowledge and belief, and they have been read over to the deponent before he signed.

H. J. Miller
Deponent.

Sworn at *London* this
10th day of *June* *1940* . before me
Walter Welc .

Officer of Customs and Excise
~~Officer of the Coastguard~~
Person appointed for the purpose
by the Board of Trade under
S. 465 of the M.S.A. 1894. } Strike out the words that do not apply.

10 JUN 1940

50

Appendix II

Reproduction of the original report by W H Simmons, Master of the tug *Cervia*, on their part in the Dunkirk evacuation and the fate of the *Royalty*. The vertical line to the left of each page is the printed margin in the book used for the report.

The tug *Cervia* in wartime grey.

1/ called upon to undertake work which will test your skill and your courage to the limit! I feel confident that these jobs will be carried out in the same spirit as before, and that you will worthily up-hold the traditions of the Mercantile Marine. I wish you all good luck. Yours Faithfully. John R. Watkins.

FRIDAY 31st MAY. Left DOVER HARBOUR at 9PM towing Sailing barge "ROYALTY" loaded with provisions, cans of fresh water and cigarettes, for the troops stranded on DUNKERQUE BEACH's. We had orders to beach the "ROYALTY" at PORT MALO about one mile east of DUNKIRK PIER HEADS. We passed through the DOWNS at midnight

SATURDAY. 1st JUNE About 1am we should have picked up the NORTH GOODWIN LT VSL, but could not find it, so set a course from the GULL LT. BUOY $SE\frac{3}{4}E$. We were in company with the tug "PERSIA" Capin H. ALDROGE, who was towing two sailing barges bound inside DUNKIRK HARBOUR. We passed over the TAIL OF SOUTH FALLS and SANDETTIE BANK and made the RUYTINGEN PASS BUOY about 5AM. altering course to SOUTH to pass the western end of the SNOUW BANK and enter DUNKERQUE RADE at N⁰ 5. W. BUOY. The tide was ebbing as we towed up through the ROADS, but progress was slow as we had to keep easing down on account of the H.M. Destroyers and Channel Packets wash as they steamed all out in a constant procession, in and away from Dunkirk Harbour. Outward bound full of troops. troops everywhere on board them. The great evacuation was on. There were a great number of wrecks about and great caution was nessasary as few were charted or buoyed. The only means of knowing where they were apart from any wreckage visable above water was the tide rip over them. We passed DUNKIRK pierheads where five H.M. Destroyers were loading up with troops, and we passed two big French destroyers that had been mined and were lying wrecked up on the beach. We shot our barge off toward the beach at 8.20am Soldiers were running down the beach to meet her, when an air raid siren began to blow ashore and the soldiers took what ever

they could find. We dropped our anchor at 8.30am, all being quiet, when over came about 15 enemy planes, with guns firing away on shore at them. Two Destroyers and a Sloop outside of us began to open fire as the planes began to bomb them, and as the Destroyers were twisting and turning at High speed to dodge the bombs, I deemed it nessasary to keep out of their way, so hove up our anchor and paddled in towards the shore, our own Lewis gun firing at the planes as they came over us. At this time our barges boat was rowing off to us, with six soldier stevedores also the master and mate of the "ROYALTY" which was now beached and anchored on the shore, Two more barge crews rowed to us in one boat and we took them all on board. The Destroyer outside of us had a stick of bombs (9) drop in the water alongside of her and they exploded under water as she kept her speed twisting and turning to dodge them, She must have been holed as she began to take a list and was getting deeper by the head. I began to run off to her, her guns firing all the time at the planes. On my way I saw a White motor life boat drifting with about 15 soldiers in it, I picked her up transfering the soldiers to us, and towing the life boat astern with the other 2 small boats, Another wave of planes came over and began to bomb the crippled Destroyer as I made my way off to her and I was forced to sheer away from her. This destroyer proved to be HMS. "KEITH". I had to keep clear of her as the Sloop was circling her at high speed in an attempt to fight off the raiders. I saw one plane brought down in a cloud of smoke, just west of the pierheads, also another destroyer there was hit by a bomb.
The big tug "ST. ABBS" was making her way to H.M.S. "KEITH" which we were standing by and by this time the KEITH had dropped her anchor and swung to the flood tide, Another tug which proved to be our "VINCIA" was running down the Roads from the eastward. The planes were still bombing the "KEITH" trying for her depth charges, but her guns failed to answer this time as the crew had been ordered to abandon her and they were dropping into the sea on rafts and spars and one or two boats, but a lot were swiming away from her on the tide, and the enemy planes made another dive at them machine gunning the men in the water, As they drove up away from

53

their ship the "VINCIA" began to pick them up and I turned round and began to run down the Roads toward the other disabled destroyer. The tug ST ABBS had got alongside the "KEITH" just as a direct hit by an enemy plane exploded the depth charges on her stern and blew the destroyer's stern right off, and I later heard that "ST ABBS" was sunk by a direct hit alongside the "KEITH." I saw a sloop hit by a bomb just north of the tug "VINCIA" and the next second a ball of fire and smoke was a thousand feet above her. I later heard this was HMS "SKIPJACK". taking ammo to the troops at DUNKIRK. Halfway to the entrance to the Harbour, I saw a sailing barge at anchor with a lot of soldiers about her decks, I went alongside of her and told them to come on board and we could leave the barge where she was, but I was told by an Army Captain that there was 250 including many badly wounded soldiers down in the hold, covered, so that enemy planes would not spot them. I put a towing spring on her bow and as they hove up the anchor, took the weight of her, but in a swell from a passing sloop, rope jerked the wooden winch from its bed and would then not heave, so began towing the barge with at least 15 fathom of chain out attached to her anchor. She was the coasting barge "TOLLESBURY". When passing the DUNKIRK PIERHEADS a Channel Steamer was just backing out loaded to capacity with troops. Another Channel packet was lying sunk on the north pierhead, I believe this was the "KING HORRY" or "GRACIE FIELDS". I saw a trawler sunk in the middle of the entrance also a twin screw tug ashore south of the pierheads. A black cloud of smoke hung over the town from the burning oil works at the western side of the town. When past the pierheads I saw that our tug "PERSIA" had taken hold of the other crippled destroyer which had been hit in No 1 Boiler room. This destroyer proved to be H.M.S. "IVANHOE." She could steam slowly, and as we with the barge in tow also "ORION IV" motor lifeboat astern of her and the "PERSIA" with her destroyer and the tug "VINCIA" with the survivors of H.M.S "KEITH" on board which included I believe Lord Gort I heard later. also the outgoing Channel steamer and an incoming packet were all jambed together rounding the No5w buoy, a shore battery just captured by the Germans began to find our range, and about twenty enemy planes came over, bombs were dropped, guns replied from all ships in the vicinity, the "IVANHOE" put up a smoke screen, and a small high speed motor launch was chasing the planes firing twin Lewis guns strait up at them. We saw nine bombs leave a plane over us and they dropped alongside the ingoing Channel Steamer, but with her helm hard over she managed to get clear of them and continued on to the Harbour. Guns were crashing all around us and a Trawler running in, let fly with all she had got. 5 Bombs were aimed at us from a plane. I could not see them or the plane as our bridge was covered with concrete. The boy F. WILDER of Gravesend. was outside the wheelhouse as all who could were jambed inside under the cover, and he told me the direction of the bombs and by sheering off hard to starboard the bombs dropped about 100 feet off our port bow, Lifting the tug bodily out of the water when they exploded, fortunately our towrope held on. One bomb was aimed at "PERSIA" but fell wide. Another was aimed at "VINCIA" but missed and the spray of it exploding washed down her decks. But we all got safely out of the Roads and when off the ROYTINGEN Buoy we were attacked again, but by this time we were on our own. The others getting away ahead of us. We now had several LEWIS guns and plenty of ammo on board with the troops we had picked up and was able to keep the planes off. Our decks were well packed with troops which we had taken on board from different small craft among them several French soldiers. On our boat deck we also had a big canoe that came alongside with two soldiers in it. When in sight of the English coast several soldiers were overcome and tears were streaming down their faces. I saw a bomb explode between a Sloop and a Destroyer that he was towing. But we all got out of it safely. When we arrived in the DOWNS about 4PM we were ordered by naval Control tug "JAVA" to proceed to RAMSGATE

5

Where we anchored in the OLD CUDD Channel. Motor boats then disembarked our troops, also took all the wounded out of the barge "TOLLESBURY" which could not be taken into the Harbour on account of the congestion in there. In all about 270 soldiers were landed from us and our tow. We were ordered to tow the barge to Gravesend.

I enquired as to what had become of a fleet of 30 French and Belgium fishermen which had spoke me early that morning on my way to DUNKIRK, who were sailing with all their families to England. I had given them a course and wished them luck. I was told that they had all arrived safely well loaded with families and troops after having sailed right over the GOODWIN SANDS on the High water. That was just one of the miracles of the evacuation.

We proceeded at 6 PM towing the barge "TOLLESBURY" "ORION IV" and two small boats. We had towed the "TOLLESBURY" across with 15 fathoms of chain out on her anchor, forgetting all about the magnectic mines. At 10 PM we dropped anchor at Southend.

SUNDAY 2nd JUNE Proceeded at daylight for Gravesend, made barge "TOLLESBURY" fast at the Ship and Lobster buoy and the "ORION IV" and two boats I handed over to Gravesend Customs.

JUNE 9th Ran to RAMSGATE, picked up two ex DUNKIRK sailing barges "BASILDON" and "ASHINGTON" bound for SOUTHEND. After passing NE SPIT buoy a magnectic mine sweeper exploded a mine alongside of us, and immediately our stern barge was adrift. We went back and picked her up and continued.

JUNE 9th Copy of Statement re S/s "EMPIRE COMMERCE"

I am Master of steam TUG "CERVIA" and have been her Master for the past 4½ years. I have been Master of TUGS on the THAMES for the past 12½ years and have had altogether 25 years experience in THAMES TUGS. The "CERVIA" is of 157 TON REGISTER 90 feet in length. 22 feet Beam. and 10 ft 6in in depth. She was built in 1925 and belongs to Messrs Wm Watkins Ltd.

CERVIA.
6

She is fitted with compound engines of 90 R.H.P. We carry a crew of 7 hands all told. In the deck department there is myself, the mate one deck hand and a boy. Below is an engineer and two firemen. We are fitted with salvage gear including a Merryweather Fire and Salvage Pump with the necessary hose and connections, ropes, wires, spare gear, anchors, etc. At about 2.10 p.m on Sunday the 9th JUNE 1940 whilst towing two sailing barges, the "BASILDON" and "ASHINGTON" bound for Southend from RAMSGATE the "CERVIA" was passing about 4 cables inside the NE SPIT Buoy when a Government Trawler engaged in mine sweeping blew up a magnectic mine on the Starboard side of "CERVIA" near the buoy and in consequence almost immediately our stern barge was adrift. We turned round on the starboard wheel and picked up the barge and left her fast on our starboard side and proceeded. At about 2.30 p.m the drifter "PLUMER" came to us and spoke us when we were approximately a mile westerly of the NE SPIT buoy, and requested us to go to the assistance of the S/S "EMPIRE COMMERCE". At the same time he stated he would take over our barges, whilst we were assisting the "EMPIRE COMMERCE". We then let go the barges and handed the same over to the charge of the "PLUMER" and proceeded to the "EMPIRE COMMERCE" which was then in tow of the Government trawler "EDWARDIAN". The "EMPIRE COMMERCE" had been mined in the stokehold, She had no steam and could not steer and she was taking heavy sheers, The "EMPIRE COMMERCE" was also without anchors and cables, The Trawler had ropes fast aft leading to the bows of the "EMPIRE COMMERCE" and whilst the "EDWARDIAN" was towing and in consequence of the heavy sheers taken by her tow from time to time the Trawler was pulled right round alongside the "EMPIRE COMMERCE" According to the direction of the sheers taken by the tow, so at times the "EDWARDIAN" fell round with her portside to the EMPIRE COMMERCE" or to the Starboard side of her tow. When the "EDWARDIAN" was in position towing ahead of the ship we proceeded up alongside her quarter and with a heavy line took the Starboard bow towrope from the stern of the Trawler and in consequence the Trawler immediately got girted

W.H. SIMMONS. (MASTER)

6

In **APPENDIX III**, three tonnages are indicated for most craft. Gross (Register) Tonnage is based on one ton for every 100 cubic feet of interior hull space. Net (Register) Tonnage is the Gross Tonnage less an allowance of one ton per 100 cubic feet of non-cargo space, ie. Master and crew's accommodation, cabin and storage space. Dead Weight Tonnage is the weight of cargo that can be carried with the legal freeboard for the intended voyage, this varying according to a formula addressing the sea conditions likely to be encountered en-route, winter and summer. The Plimsoll Line, or Load Line on the side of the vessel indicates the various limits applicable to that particular craft.

APPENDIX III

Vessels Mentioned during the conversation with Capt Henry Miller BEM

Craft listed in alphabetical order. The data is compiled from Official Records. Additional notes on certain craft detail information on history, construction, ultimate fate, etc.

Sailing Barge *Adriatic*
Off. No. 112756   Port of Registry London (No.143 in 1900)
Built Beverly, Yorkshire, 1900, by J Scarr   Steel construction
Net Tonnage: 61   Gross Tonnage: 77 under sail   Dead Weight: 135 as advertised
Rig, Topsail   Dimensions 79.7 feet x 19 feet x 5.6 feet
Original Owner: H Keep (London)
By 1911   T Scholey (London)
By 1951   Upnor Sand Company
By 1957   Hardinge   Motor Barge 1958
Commenced trading under Capt Henry Miller 9th September 1900, passage Margate to London; 2001 hulked Hoo, Kent.

Sailing Barge *Aidie*
Off. No. 145839   Port of Registry Ipswich (No.2 in 1925)
Built Brightlingsea, Essex, 1924 (per Lloyds 1925), by Aldous Successors   Steel construction
Net Tonnage: 119   Gross Tonnage: 144   Dead Weight: 200 Tons
Rig, Mule, Type, Coasting   Dimensions 93 feet x 22.7 feet x 7.7 feet
Original Owner: R & W Paul (Ipswich)
Voyage 1/6/1940 to British Expeditionary Force, Dunkirk, Master Henry Potter, abandoned on Naval Orders, crew safe; 1941 compensation of £3,490 paid to R & W Paul; 1949 reported as coaling hulk, Dunkirk Harbour.

Sailing Barge *Alan*
Off. No. 112679   Port of Registry London (No.43 in 1900)
Built Battersea, London, 1900, by H Keep
Net Tonnage: 61   Gross Tonnage: 85   Dead Weight: 155 tons to sea (1908)
                                                                                     160 tons - advertisement 1911
Rig, Topsail   Dimensions 82 feet x 20.8 feet x 6.6 feet
Original Owner: H Keep (London), 1911 sold at auction, Gravesend
By 1911   London & Rochester Trading Company
1947 engine fitted; houseboat 1963 - 1976 below M2 Medway Bridge, 2001 houseboat Hoo, Kent.

Sailing Barge *Alf Everard*
Off. No. 148691   Port of Registry London
Built Gt Yarmouth, Norfolk, 1925, by J H Fellows   Steel construction
Net Tonnage: 149   Gross Tonnage: 190   Dead Weight: 300 tons as built
Rig, Mule, Type, Coasting   Dimensions 97.6 feet x 23.1 feet x 9.6 feet
Original Owner: F T Everard (Greenhithe)
By 6/1943 rebuilt as Motor Ship, engine fitted, sailing gear removed, voyage 24/12/1953 Charlestown, Par to London with China Clay at 6.30pm sunk in collision with *City of Johannesburg* east of Nore Tower.

Sailing Barge *Anglo American*

Off. No. 115854   Port of Registry London (No.123 in 1902)

Built Greenhithe, Kent, 1902, by F T Eberhardt

Net Tonnage: 67   Gross Tonnage: 93.15   Dead Weight: 165 Tons

Rig, Mule, Type, Coasting   Dimensions 85.5 feet x 22.2 feet x 6.92 feet

Original Owner: F T Eberhardt (Greenhithe) (Mortgaged to Laura Ann Doe)

By 1902   Lanno & Sanson (Portland) (4/9/1902)

By 1902   H J Sanson (Bath Stone Company, Portland) (11/10/1902)

Voyage 4/11/1915 Portland to Alderney, at 12.45am struck Alderney breakwater in thick fog, crew abandoned the vessel and landed safely; 6/11/1915 barge located stranded east of Hope's Nose, 3 miles east of Torquay, badly holed, Total Loss, Registry closed 29/11/1915. NB Sister barge to *Britisher*.

A dramatic photograph of the Battersea, London built *Baltic* on the rocks of St Clement's Isle off Mousehole in Cornwall in 1907. Deep laden with a cargo of cement from the Isle of Wight, she miraculously survived and after repairs traded on until sunk in Milton Creek, Kent.

Sailing Barge *Arctic*

Off. No. 108227   Port of Registry London (No.92 in 1897, No.111 in 1898, No.100 in 1913 as Motor Vessel)

Built Greenwich, London, 28/6/1897, by J Rennie, rebuilt Greenwich, London, 1898, by J Rennie Iron construction

Net Tonnage: 68   Gross Tonnage: 86   Dead Weight: 145 (as motor barge 1913)

Rig, Topsail   Dimensions 78.6 feet x 19.1 feet x 4.8 feet (As built 1897)

        Dimensions 85.5 feet x 19.1 feet x 6.7 feet (As rebuilt 1898)

Original Owner: H Keep (London), 1911 offered at auction, Gravesend, sold 1913

Voyage 27/3/1900 recorded London to Margate with Coal, under Master Henry Miller

1913 - 1963   London & Rochester Barge Company, engine fitted, sails removed

1988 - 2001 Fulham as housebarge.

Sailing Barge *Atlantic*

Off. No. 89599   Port of Registry London (No.115 in 1884)
Built East Greenwich, London, 1884, by Pascoe & Wright Iron construction
Net Tonnage: 69   Gross Tonnage: 77   Dead Weight: 130 as advertised 1911
Rig, Topsail   Dimensions 84.2 feet x 18.5 feet x 6.3 feet
Original Owner: A Keep (90 Lower Thames Street, London)
By 1900   A H Keep (90 Lower Thames Street, London) (Advertised for sale 1910)
By 1919   H A Crampton (Portsmouth)
By 1921   T E Ward (Gravesend)
Voyage 27/8/1923 Fowey to Port Audemer with China Clay, under Master Tremain, struck buoy in River Rille and sank; salvage possible but not advised owing to age and condition.

Sailing Barge *Avon*

Probably an unregistered 'stumpie' barge - no record found.

Sailing Barge *Baltic*

Off. No. 102792   Port of Registry London (No.99 in 1893)
Built Battersea, London, 1893, by H Keep
Net Tonnage: 55   Gross Tonnage: 70.70   Dead Weight: 160 tons - advertisement
Rig, Topsail   Dimensions 82 feet x 19.3 feet x 6.1 feet
Original Owner: H Keep (London)
By 1911   Charles Burley (Sittingbourne) (23/3/1911)
1/11/1907 Newport, Isle of Wight to Newlyn with Cement, Master Langford, with wife and daughter aboard, Mate George Baines, reported wrecked 'Mousehole Island' (St Clement's Isle) 2 miles from Newlyn, all on board saved, barge repaired. 16/12/1910 London to Gt Yarmouth with wheat, assisted by the Harwich lifeboat in gale. Sunk by collision at anchor outside Milton Creek, laid up Milton Creek, derelict 1935, Registry closed 12/3/1936, broken up and remains buried Churchfield, west bank, Milton Creek, Kent.

Sailing Barge *Barbara Jean*

Off. No. 149251   Port of Registry Ipswich (No.4 in 1925)
Built Brightlingsea, Essex, 1924 (per Lloyds Oct 1925), by Aldous Successors   Steel construction
Net Tonnage: 119   Gross Tonnage: 144   Dead Weight: 200 Tons
Rig, Mule, Type, Coasting   Dimensions 93 feet x 22.2 feet x 7.7 feet
Original Owner: R & W Paul (Ipswich)
Voyage 1/6/1940 to British Expeditionary Force, Dunkirk, Master Charlie Webb, abandoned on beach and blown up after unloading stores, crew safe.

Sailing Barge *Britannia*

Off. No. 87115   Port of Registry London (No.18 in 1883)
Built Milton, Kent, 5/1883, by R M Shrubsall
Net Tonnage: 45   Gross Tonnage: Dead Weight 110 Tons burden (press report)
Rig, Stumpie 1883, Topsail by 1887 (Thames Match)   Dimensions 78.4 feet x 17.4 feet x 5.4 feet
Original Owner: C Stone (Northfleet)
By 1899   J C Neill (Manager) J Stone (Northfleet)
By 1919   Anderson (Maidstone)
Voyage 1/1924 at Broad Ness with timber, in collision, Constructive Total Loss, Registry closed 10/1924.

Sailing Barge *Britisher*

Off. No. 115802   Port of Registry London (No.67 in 1902)

Built Greenhithe, Kent, 1902, by F T Eberhardt

Net Tonnage: 68   Gross Tonnage: 94.61 Dead Weight: 165 Tons

Rig, Mule, Type, Coasting   Dimensions 87 feet x 22.2 feet x 6.9 feet

Original Owner: F T Eberhardt (Greenhithe)

then   F T Everard (Greenhithe)

Voyage 4/11/1941 Norwich to London reported with empty ammunition boxes (described Bottle Cases by Lloyds), Master Harry Delaney, struck mine near N E Maplin Buoy, 2 crew lost. NB Sister barge to *Anglo American*.

The *Cambria* lies at Greenhithe, her birthplace, in 1963, almost half a century on and still trading under the Everard flag. She was sold to her skipper, A W 'Bob' Roberts, who continued to trade with her, the last commercial carrier under sail in northern europe, until 1970. Captain Roberts wrote many books about his experiences afloat, and the *Cambria* went on to become one of the most photographed and filmed of all the sailing barges, even having a television drama series based on her last years in trade. Taken over by the Maritime Trust for preservation, her condition rapidly deteriorated and efforts to restore this important vessel and ensure her future have struggled to gain the needed funding. Her future remains uncertain, though a new trust has been formed in the hope of securing the necessary resources.

Sailing Barge *Briton*

Off. No. 114752   Port of Registry London (No.187 in 1901)
Built Greenhithe, Kent, 1901, by F T Eberhardt
Net Tonnage: 65   Gross Tonnage: 82   Dead Weight: 135 Tons to sea
Rig, Topsail   Dimensions 85 feet x 20.2 feet x 6.4 feet
Original Owner: Wm T Clifford (73 Lower Thames Street, London)
By 1910   F T Eberhardt (Greenhithe)
Later   F T Everard (Greenhithe)
Voyage 20/12/1923 Boston to Sandwich with Coal, stranded in strong north wind on Blakeney West Beach, Lifeboat saved crew, cargo washing out of hold and barge breaking up, 24/12/1923 reported barge and cargo totally lost, deck and quarter gone, Registry closed 11/11/1924.

Sailing Barge *Cambria*

Off. No. 120676   Port of Registry London (No.36 in 1906)
Built Greenhithe, Kent, 1906, by W Eberhardt (Launched same day as Hibernia)
Net Tonnage: 79   Gross Tonnage: 109.29   Dead Weight: 175 tons to sea
Rig, Mule, Type, Coasting   Dimensions 91.1 feet x 21.9 feet x 7.3 feet
Original Owner: F T Eberhardt
By 1907   H Keep (4/1/1907)
By 1908   W Eberhardt (5/11/1908) later F T Everard
By 1966   Alfred Wm Roberts (13/1/1966)
By 1971   The Maritime Trust
By 1975 preserved open to the public at Rochester Esplanade, relocated to St Katherine Dock, London, in Maritime Trust Collection; collection dispersed, moved 1987 to Dolphin Sailing Barge Museum, Sittingbourne, in poor condition, dedicated trust established 2000 to rescue and restore vessel subject to availability of funding; Last pure sailing vessel to carry cargo in northern europe.

Tug *Cervia, ex Tamesa*

Off. No. 148586   Port of Registry London
Built South Shields, Tyne & Weir, 1925, by J P Rennoldson & Son   Steel construction
     Gross Tonnage: 157   Engine: 90 HP
     Dimensions 90.0 feet x 22.0 feet x 10.6 feet
Original Owner: United Steam Tug Company
By 1937   William Watkins Limited (London and Gravesend), name changed to *Cervia*
By 1946   Ridley Tugs, Newcastle, name changed to *Monty*
By 1954   J H Pigott, Grimsby, name changed to *Lady Elsie*
1962 renamed *Lady Hazel*, 1963 scrapped Holland.

Sailing Barge *City of London*

Off. No. 82780   Port of Registry London (No.83 in 1880)
Built East Greenwich, London, 1880, by A D Lewis   Iron construction, wooden decks
Net Tonnage: 55   Gross Tonnage: 67   Dead Weight: 130 as advertised
Rig, Topsail   Dimensions 81.0 feet x 18.8 feet x 5.9 feet
Original Owner: A Keep (Lower Thames Street, London)
By 1900   A H Keep (Lower Thames Street, London)
By 1919   E J & W Goldsmith
Registry closed 1929 Broken up at Grays, Essex.

Composite Clipper Ship *Cutty Sark*

Built Dumbarton, Scotland, 1869, by Scott & Linton to design of Hercules Linton

Net Tonnage: 921   Gross Tonnage: 963   Underdeck: 892 Tons

Type, Tea Clipper   Dimensions 212.5 feet x 36 feet x 21 feet

Composite construction of timber on iron frames.

Original Owner: Captain John Willis (London)

Designed and built to beat *Thermopylae* in the tea trade from China, *Cutty Sark* made many fast passages from both China and with wool from Australia; from 1895 to 1922 sailed under the Portuguese flag under the name *Ferreira*; in 1922 purchased by Captain Dowman and brought to Falmouth where reconditioned and re-rigged; by 1938 presented to the Thames Nautical Training College and laid abreast of the *Worcester* off Greenhithe; vessel handed over to the Cutty Sark Preservation Society in 1953; entered dry dock at Greenwich in 1954 for refit for permanent static display; in 1957 opened to the public by Her Majesty The Queen.

Sailing Barge *Cygnet*

Off. No. 87118   Port of Registry London (No.121 in 1883)

Built Swanscombe, Kent, 1883, by J Bazley White

Net Tonnage: 57   Gross Tonnage: 57   Dead Weight: when new 140 Tons, later 130 Tons

Rig, Topsail   Dimensions 83.0 feet x 18.6 feet x 5.6 feet

Original Owner: J Bazley White (Swanscombe)

By 1901   A P C M

Registry closed 8/1930, by 1933 hulk at Upnor APCM Yard; broken up c.1960 Rochester Castle Esplanade.

Sailing Barge *Dabchick*

Off. No. 89670   Port of Registry London (No.25 in 1885)

Built Swanscombe, Kent, 1885, by J Bazley White

Net Tonnage: 62   Gross Tonnage: 70   Dead Weight: 130 Tons

Rig, Topsail   Dimensions 84.0 feet x 19.2 feet x 5.9 feet

Original Owner: J Bazley White (Swanscombe)

By 1901   A P C M

By 1931   A Hills (Greenwich)

Registry closed 1948, hulk 1950, Lying derelict Temple Yacht Club, Strood 1951, broken up 1951.

Sailing Barge *Daisy Little*

Off. No. 98797   Port of Registry Rochester (No.4 in 1891)

Built Strood, Kent, 1891 (launched 12/1890)(cost £950), by G H Curel

Net Tonnage: 50   Gross Tonnage: 59   Dead Weight: 109 Tons

Rig, Topsail   Dimensions 81 feet x 17.5 feet x 5.5 feet

Original Owner: J Little (Strood)

By 1896   H Keep (London)

By 1903   C Cancellor (Higham)

By 1906   A Keep (London)

By 1922   Mrs A (Agnes) M Little (Strood) Managed by James Little

By 1934   Gillingham Portland Cement Company

By 2/1940 hulked at Gillingham Cement Works, 6/1941 sold and converted to mooring lifting vessel at Gravesend

By 1947   T G Spice (Gravesend)

Vessel broken up Gravesend, c. 1950. Note PLA record shows owners 20/5/1897 as Harry Keep, Ada Keep and Cecil Arthur Cancellor at 90 Lower Thames Street, London, trading as Alfred H Keep. Record cancelled 5/8/1904 and changed to Alfred H Keep - Harry Keep, managing director (name crossed out), George Holyoake Frow (Sec.).

Sailing Barge *Doffoly*
Off. No. 110102   Port of Registry London (No.93 in 1899)
Built Greenhithe, Kent, 1898, by F T Eberhardt
Net Tonnage: 55   Gross Tonnage: 80   Dead Weight: 135 Tons
Rig, Topsail   Dimensions 84.3 feet x 20.2 feet x 6.1 feet
Original Owner: H Keep (London)
1899 trading London, Broadstairs, Margate, Ramsgate, under Capt Peartree. 2/6/1903 Lloyds Weekly Ship Index - London to Southampton with Wheat, struck the 'Dries' (rocks) at 1.30 p.m. Drifted off and sank in six fathoms, Selsey Bill bearing NE 1.5 miles, Total Loss.

Sailing Barge *Ethel Everard*
Off. No. 149723   Port of Registry London
Built Gt Yarmouth, Norfolk, 1926, by J H Fellows   Steel construction
Net Tonnage: 156   Gross Tonnage: 190   Dead Weight: 300 tons maximum
Rig, Mule, Type, Coasting   Dimensions 97.6 feet x 23.1 feet x 9.6 feet
Original Owner: F T Everard (Greenhithe)
Voyage 31/5/1940 towed by tug *Sun XII* with SB *Tollesbury* to British Expeditionary Force, Dunkirk, WWII, Master Tom Willis, 1/6/1940 beached and abandoned at La Panne, France, crew taken off.

Alf Everard (left) of 1925 and *Ethel Everard,* built 1926, seen here on a company postcard. As with many companies in the coastal trade at that time, F T Everard & Sons had a London office, from which many of the 'orders' were issued, in addition to their riverside premises.

Sailing Barge *Ethel Margetts*

Off. No. 76617   Port of Registry Rochester (No.30 in 1877)

Built Strood (Upper Yard), Kent, 26/6/1877, by G H Curel

Net Tonnage: 48 as built, 42 later (1901)   Dead Weight: 85 Tons (89 Tons by 1912)

Rig, Topsail, Type, River   Dimensions 75.2 feet x 16.1 feet x 5.5 feet

Original Owner: W Margetts of West Kent Gault Brick & Cement Company

By 1902   West Kent Portland Cement Company

By 1912   B P C M (Transfer)

0830 hours 13/1/1915 sunk in collision with SS Gannet near Ovens Buoy, raised, repaired and returned to service.

By 1932   Wadhams & Smeed (£9)

Registry closed 1932, in use as Clubhouse by 1935, derelict 1958, broken up at Kettles Yard, Chatham, Kent, 1975.

From the 5/4/1891 Census, Ethel Margetts age 20, a clerk, daughter of William G Margetts, cement manufacturer, residing with family at Rings Hill Lodge, Wouldham, Kent.

Sailing Barge *Fortis*

Off. No. 109922   Port of Registry Rochester (No.19 in 1898)

Built Gt Yarmouth, Norfolk, 1898, by H Fellows   Steel construction

Net Tonnage: 53   Gross Tonnage: 66   Dead Weight: 125 Tons

Rig, Topsail   Dimensions 81 feet x 19.2 feet x 5.7 feet

Original Owner: G Watson (Rochester)

By 1914   J R Piper

By ?   T Scholey

Sailed 9/1951 London to Maldon light, de-rigged on arrival and used for timber lightering by new owner Sadds of Maldon; 1961 vessel cut up at Maldon.

Sailing Barge *Giralda*

Off. No. 108210   Port of Registry London (No.84 in 1897)

Built Greenwich, London, 1897, by J R Piper

Net Tonnage: 49.73 (as built) 54 (later)   Gross Tonnage: 68.71   Dead Weight: 130 Tons

Rig, Topsail, Type, Built for racing   Dimensions 83.8 feet x 18.8 feet x 6.0 feet

Original Owner: E J & W Goldsmith (Grays)

By 1897   J R Piper (22/10/1897)

By 1899   F Lambert (London)

By 1913   Cory Lighterage (26/10/1913)

Voyage 22/10/1927 sunk in collision with steamer, Gravesend Reach, raised and used as roads barge, Registry closed 29/11/27, later broken up c.1945 Tilbury.

Auxiliary Ketch Barge *Grit I*

Off. No. 135249   Port of Registry London

Built Greenhithe, Kent, 7/1913, by F T Everard

Net Tonnage: 79   Gross Tonnage: 147   Dead Weight: 200

Rig, Ketch, Type, Wood Auxiliary Coasting   Dimensions 94 feet x 23 feet x 8.9 feet

Original Owner: F T Everard (Greenhithe)

Voyage 21/10/1916, for Le Havre, France, with military stores (WWI), when 25 miles south of Beachy Head, sunk by gunfire from German submarine (UB29), Total Loss.

Auxiliary Ketch Barge *Grit II*

Off. No. 147531　　　Port of Registry London
Built Greenhithe, Kent, 8/1923, by F T Everard
Net Tonnage: 110　　Gross Tonnage: 193　　　　Dead Weight: 250 Tons
Wood Motor Vessel (Extra Ketch Rig Sails), 4 cyl oil engine, Plenty & Son
　　　　　　　　　Dimensions 105.8 feet x 23.5 feet x 8.9 feet
Original Owner:　　　F T Everard (Greenhithe)
Voyage 22/2/1934 Keadby to Exeter with Coal, sunk in collision (Fog) with the Latvian Steamer *Gaisma* off Hythe, Total Loss.

Sailing Barge *Harold Margetts*

Off. No. 97717　　　Port of Registry Rochester (No.6 in 1890)
Built Frindsbury, Kent, 1890, by G H Curel
Net Tonnage: 45　　Gross Tonnage: 59.47　Dead Weight: 110 Tons
Rig, Topsail, Type, River　　Dimensions 77.5 feet x 17.6 feet x 5.5 feet
Original Owner:　　　West Kent Portland Cement Company
By 1912　　　　　　B P C M (Transfer)
By 1933　　　　　　G Andrews (Sittingbourne) for £150
By 1938　　　　　　Gillett (Faversham)
Dead heated with *Plinlimmon* in 1927 Medway Barge Sailing Match; 26/1/1935, with Thames Ballast, Master Edward Thomas Wellard of Sittingbourne, Mate Alfred Ratcliff of Faversham, foundered in NW gale in the Nore Swatch, both drowned, bodies found in cabin when barge raised and taken to Rosherville, Kent; converted to barge yacht in 1947, derelict on the Norfolk Broads by 1976.

Sailing Barge *Haughty Belle*

Off. No. 105843　　　Port of Registry London (No.90 in 1896)
Built East Greenwich, London, 1896, by J R Piper
Net Tonnage: 53　　Gross Tonnage: 68
Rig, Topsail　　　　Dimensions 83 feet x 19.5 feet x 5.9 feet
Original Owner:　　　E J & W Goldsmith (Grays)
By 1933 sold for conversion to barge yacht (owner not known), 1937 30 HP engine fitted, by 1955 hulked at Cubitt's Yacht Basin, broken up at Chiswick Quay, remains buried by 1970s.

Sailing Barge *Her Majesty*

Off. No. 109106　　　Port of Registry Ramsgate
Built Sittingbourne, Kent, 1897, by A White
Net Tonnage: 53　　Gross Tonnage: 62　　Dead Weight: 120 Tons
Type, Hoy Barge; Rig, Topsail　　Dimensions 82.0 feet x 18.7 feet x 5.7 feet
Original Owner:　　　Margate Hoy Company
By 1918　　　　　　F T Everard (Greenhithe)
1920 trading London to Calais and Boulogne, under Capt J Mole. Houseboat 1947, broken up at Chiswick Quay.

Sailing Barge *Heron*

Off. No. 110174   Port of Registry London (No.188 in 1899)
Built Greenhithe, Kent, 1899, by F T Eberhardt
Net Tonnage: 64   Gross Tonnage: 87   Dead Weight: 160 Tons
Rig, Topsail   Dimensions 83.6 feet x 20.1 feet x 6.3 feet
Original Owner: Bevan (Northfleet)
By 1902   A P C M
By 1927   E J Butcher (Orpington) (£745)
By ?   A E Scholey
By 1947 converted to barge yacht, 1978 derelict at Penpre Creek, River Fal, 1980 hulk in use as jetty/breakwater River Fal.

Hibernia leaves her River Trent berth empty, and under tow. Her laden waterline for her last freight is clearly identified by the water mark left behind on her hull. The Everard craft dominated the sailing barge trade between London and the Trent wharves.

Sailing Barge *Hibernia*

Off. No. 120677   Port of Registry London (No.37 in 1906)
Built Greenhithe, Kent, 1906, by F T Eberhardt (Launched same day as *Cambria*)
Net Tonnage: 79   Gross Tonnage: 109.29   Dead Weight: 175 tons to sea
Rig, Mule, Type, Coasting   Dimensions 91.1 feet x 21.9 feet x 7.3 feet
Original Owner: F T Eberhardt
By 1907   Half share to H Keep (4/1/1907)
By 1908   W Eberhardt (5/11/1908) later F T Everard
Voyage 10/11/1937 Goole to Sittingbourne with Gas Coal, Master H Couchman; abandoned, crew taken off by Cromer Lifeboat, barge went ashore at Runton, Nr Cromer, total wreck.

Sailing Barge *John Bayly*

Off. No. 104760   Port of Registry Ramsgate (No.6 in 1895)

Built Sandwich, Kent, 1895, by W Felton

Net Tonnage: 56   Gross Tonnage: 66   Dead Weight: 120 Tons

Type, Hoy Barge; Rig, Topsail   Dimensions 81.2 feet x 18.7 feet x 5.6 feet

Original Owner: Margate Hoy Company

By 1918   A M Everard

Registry closed 1937, broken up July 1937 at Greenhithe.

Sailing Barge *Lady Mary*

Off. No. 112692   Port of Registry London (No.58 in 1900)

Built Greenhithe, Kent, 1900, by F T Eberhardt

Net Tonnage: 49   Gross Tonnage: 67   Dead Weight: 125 tons

Rig, Topsail   Dimensions 84.5 feet x 18.6 feet x 5.9 feet

Original Owner: Charles Charleton (Greenhithe)

By 1915   F T Everard (Greenhithe)

By 1957   Thames Barge Sailing Club (£1) (12/8/1957)

Taken over by Erith Yacht Club, de-rigged, became spar store moored by Erith Yacht Club's light-ship headquarters, by 1966 spars and rigging used for restoration of SB *Kathleen* by Richard Walsh, hulked early 1970s at Erith. NB Chas. Charleton was Director of Johnson's Cement Works, Greenhithe.

Sailing Barge *Lady Maud*

Off. No. 118305   Port of Registry London (No.122 in 1903)

Built Greenhithe, Kent, 1903, by F T Eberhardt

Net Tonnage: 59   Gross Tonnage: 76.25   Dead Weight: 135 Tons

Rig, Topsail   Dimensions 84 feet x 20 feet x 5.9 feet

Original Owner: Charles Charleton (Greenhithe)

By 1922   F T Everard (Greenhithe) (7/9/1922)

Hulk by c.1958, broken up, 1970 Registry closed. NB Chas. Charleton was Director of Johnson's Cement Works, Greenhithe.

Sailing Barge *Lord Kitchener*

Off. No. 110073   Port of Registry London (No.57 in 1899)

Built Greenhithe, Kent, 1899, by F T Eberhardt

Net Tonnage: 56.25 Gross Tonnage: 79.57   Dead Weight: 130 Tons to sea

Rig, Topsail, Type, Coasting   Dimensions 84 feet x 20.4 feet x 6.0 feet

Original Owner: F T Eberhardt (Greenhithe)

By 1925   F T Everard (Greenhithe)

Voyage 17/1/1926 Poole to Par, light, Master James Stow, wrecked Redlap Cove, 3 miles west of Dartmouth, 2 crew, Herbert Ambrose and Charles McCann, lost, Captain Stow survived, Registry closed 4/2/1926.

Sailing Barge *Lina, ex Essex*

Off. No. 114768   Port of Registry London (No.205 in 1901)

Built Sweden, 1901, by Bergquava Syndicate

Net Tonnage: 63   Gross Tonnage: 78   Dead Weight 140 Tons

Rig, Gaff as built, changed to Topsail   Dimensions 83.4 feet x 19.8 feet x 5.7 feet

Original Owner: Bergquava Syndicate (London, Broad Street, City)
By 1906   Mrs S A Eberhardt (Greenhithe)
By 1911   F T Everard (23/3/1911)
NB Built with caulked sides; 2105 hours 17/11/1938, with Cement, sunk in collision with Danish SS *Henry Tegner* in Blackwall Reach, off Enderby's Wharf, Greenwich; 1415 hours 18/11/1938, raised and taken to Greenhithe, declared Constructive Total Loss, laid up Greenhithe, 1939 yard roads barge; Registry closed 16/6/1939; 1953 broken up by owner at Greenhithe.

Sailing Barge *Marguerite, ex Surrey*
Off. No. 114608   Port of Registry London (No.252 in 1901)
Built Sweden, 1901, by Bergquava Syndicate
Net Tonnage: 63   Gross Tonnage: 77   Dead Weight: 140 Tons
Rig, Gaff as built, changed to Topsail   Dimensions 83 feet x 19.0 feet x 5.8 feet
Original Owner: Bergquava Syndicate (London, Broad Street, City)
By 1906   Mrs S A Eberhardt (Greenhithe)
By 1911   F T Everard (23/3/1911)
NB Built with caulked sides, 1918 - 1921 trading to Continent, Master Henry Miller, 1946 laid up, 1953 Registry closed, broken up by owner.

Sailing Barge *Minnie*
Off. No. 43995   Port of Registry London (No.19 in 1862)
Built Portsmouth, Hampshire, 1861, by unknown builder
Net Tonnage: 46   Gross Tonnage: 46   Deadweight: 96 Tons
Rig, Topsail   Dimensions 73.1 feet x 17.8 feet x 5.6 feet
Original Owner: John Charleton (25 Gt Tower Street, London)
By 1917   F T Everard (Greenhithe),
Sailed in second Thames Match 1864, Master Wm Waghorn, Registry closed 1925, mooring hulk, broken up.

Tug *Muria, ex Wrestler, ex Hotspur*
Off. No. 136308   Port of Registry London (1920)
Built Bowling, Scotland, 1914, by Scott & Sons   Steel construction
                         Gross Tonnage: 192   Engine: 90 HP
Original Owner: Steel & Bennie (Glasgow) as *Wrestler*
By 1918   Royal Navy, name changed to *Hotspur*
By 1920   William Watkins (London and Gravesend), name changed to *Muria*
8/11/1940, mined off North Foreland.

Sailing Barge *New York*
Off. No. 77108   Port of Registry London (No.67 in 1878)
Built Greenhithe, Kent, 1878, by A Keep
Net Tonnage: 54   Gross Tonnage: 61   Dead Weight: 115 Tons
Rig, Topsail   Dimensions 79.6 feet x 18.1 feet x 6.0 feet
Original Owner: A Keep (City)
By 1901   W R Cunis Limited
Registry closed 1933, broken up.

Sailing Barge *New Zealand*

Off. No. 82777   Port of Registry London (No.80 in 1880)
                        Port of Registry Cowes (1921)
Built Greenhithe, Kent, 1879, by A Keep
Net Tonnage: 64   Gross Tonnage: 70   Dead Weight: 130 Tons
Net Tonnage: 41 (1934)
Rig, Topsail   Dimensions 81.9 feet x 18.5 feet x 6.6 feet
Original Owner: A Keep (City)
By 1901   William Lionel Wyllie (Hoo)
By 1934 as *Louisa*   Cowes Steam Tug & Transport Company
Converted to yacht for celebrated marine artist W L Wyllie, renamed *Four Brothers*, later *Gwalia*, later *Louisa* (1921) engined 50 BHP, eventually derelict Nr Cowes, IOW, broken up.

Liner *Orion*

Off. No. 164493   Port of Registry London
Built Barrow-in-Furness, Cumbria, 1935, by Vickers-Armstrong   Steel construction
                        Gross Tonnage: 23,696
Twin Screw, Geared Turbine, 20 knots
Original Owner: Orient Steam Navigation Company
By 1939   Requisitioned as Troopship for WWII
By 1947   Resumed civilian service on England-Australia run
By 1960   Transferred to P & O
In 1963 withdrawn from service and chartered as Hotel Ship in Hamburg; later same year scrapped; *Orion's* ships bell in use as church bell at Christ Church, Thorpe Bay, Essex.

Sailing Barge *Pacific*

Off. No. 89606   Port of Registry London (No.112 in 1884)
Built East Greenwich, London, 1884, by Pascoe & Wright Iron or steel construction
Net Tonnage: 69   Gross Tonnage: 77   Dead Weight: 130 tons - advertisement (1885)
              60 (1937)
Rig, Topsail   Dimensions 84.2 feet x 18.5 feet x 6.3 feet
Original Owner: A H Keep
By 1911   J R Piper
By 1919   H Crampton (Portsmouth)
By 1922   J G Hammond (City)
By 1934   Batchelor (Halling)
By 1945   Whiting Bros
Engine fitted 1936/7, condemned 1948 - broken up.

Sailing Barge *Plinlimmon*

Off. No. 91902   Port of Registry London (No.17 in 1886)
Built Strood, Kent, 1886, by G H Curel
Net Tonnage: 57 as built, 45 later   Gross Tonnage: 57   Dead Weight: 110 Tons
Rig, Topsail, Type, River   Dimensions 78.2 feet x 17.6 feet x 5.3 feet
Original Owner: E W & W H Brooks (Grays)
By 1900   Hilton Anderson & Brooks (Halling)
By 1902   A P C M
Dead heated with *Harold Margetts* in 1927 Medway Barge Sailing Match; in 1930s sold for £225

for conversion to barge yacht, 22/9/1935 steering gear failed, towed into Newhaven with six persons on board including author, playwright and M P, A P Herbert, still on Register 1947.

Sailing Barge *Plover*
Off. No. 110026   Port of Registry London (No.240 in 1898)
Built Swanscombe, Kent, 1898, by J Bazley White
Net Tonnage: 62   Gross Tonnage: 76   Dead Weight: 135 Tons
Rig, Topsail   Dimensions 86.0 feet x 19.3 feet x 5.5 feet
Original Owner: J Bazley White (Swanscombe)
By 1902   A P C M
By 1933   S J Brice (Rochester) (1/4/1933) for £250
Registry closed 5/1952, houseboat 1952, hulk Whitewall Creek.

Sailing Barge *Princess*
Off. No. 116171   Port of Registry Harwich (No.4 in 1902)
Built East Greenwich, 12/1902, by H Shrubsall
Net Tonnage: 58   Gross Tonnage: 74   Dead Weight: 130 Tons
Rig, Topsail   Dimensions 85.3 feet x 19.2 feet x 6.3 feet
Original Owner: R R Horlock (Mistley)
By 1919   H F Horlock & Partners (Mistley)
By 1935   F T Everard (Greenhithe) for £375 (8/7/1935)
Hulked and derelict at Greenhithe by 1946, Registry closed 3/1953, broken up.

Sailing Barge *Ready*
Off. No. 96485   Port of Registry Maldon
Built Maldon, 1892, by J Howard
Net Tonnage: 49   Gross Tonnage: 64.03   Dead Weight: 115 Tons - would load 500
                                                 Quarters Wheat = 112.5 Tons
Rig, Topsail (stackie) Dimensions 82 feet x 20.9 feet x 5.9 feet
Original Owner: W W Keeble (Maldon)
By 1925   C Pudney (Maldon)
By 1935   Francis & Gilders (Colchester)
By 1945 re-named *Mirosa*, original name transferred to Trinity House tender; sold to Brown & Son, Chelmsford, hull stripped for timber lightering Osea Island to Heybridge Basin; Sold to C A Duvall 1965, re-rigged; currently owned (since 1976) by Peter Dodds, never engined, still in service 2001.

Sailing Barge *Redwing*
Off. No. 79893   Port of Registry Rochester (No.16 in 1879)
Built Erith, Kent, 1879, by Stone
Net Tonnage: 53   Gross Tonnage: 60   Dead Weight: 110 tons - advertisement
Rig, Topsail   Dimensions 80.9 feet x 18.4 feet x 5.4 feet
Original Owner: F Raikes (Gentleman)
By 1885   C Colwell (Vauxhall)
By 1902   A H Keep
By 1911   C Burley
Derelict 1939, declared Constructive Total Loss 29/11/1944, Registry closed 1947, burnt 1949/1950 at Shaw's Wharf, Rainham, Kent.

Sailing Barge *Royalty*

Off. No. 109919   Port of Registry Rochester (No.16 in 1898)

Built Rochester, Kent, 1898, by W Highams

Net Tonnage: 85   Gross Tonnage: 101   Dead Weight: 165 Tons to sea, 200 Tons in river

Rig, Mule. Originally large river barge, converted 1917 to Coaster

Original Owner: W Haymen (Rochester)

By 1907   G Watson (2/1907)

By 1907   F T Everard (14/5/1907)

Abandoned at Malo les Bains, near Dunkirk, France 1/6/1940, Master Henry Miller - blown up.

The Maldon registered *Ready* seen here in October 1937. Although a little shy of a really good fit, her topsail is mitre cut, enabling the sailmaker to improve the shape of the sail, though usually a more expensive method of manufacture than conventional panels parallel to the leach. *Ready* was re-named *Mirosa* in 1945. She has been privately owned by Peter Dodds for a quarter of a century, regularly in commission, and through his commitment is undoubtedly one of the finest wooden barges surviving today. She is still without an engine.

The *Royalty* ashore. The circumstances of this photograph are uncertain. The wind-filled bunts in her stowed mainsail indicate a fresh onshore breeze, the topsail has been dropped on the wrong side of the mast in a bit of a tangle, her leeboard appears embedded in the beach, and the heap of sand alongside appears to have been shovelled out of her hold, unusual if unloading, which would normally have been directly into carts, as the incoming tide could otherwise wash some of the cargo away. Perhaps she is there through stress of weather.

Sailing Barge, *Sara*

Off. No. 115858   Port of Registry London (No.128 in 1902)

Built Conyer, Kent, 8/1902, by A White

Net Tonnage: 50   Gross Tonnage: 67.62   Dead Weight: 115 Tons

Rig, Topsail   Dimensions 84.6 feet x 18.9 feet x 5.8 feet

Original Owner: S H Horlock (Mistley) (25/8/1902)

By 1921   A H Horlock (Mistley) for £815

By 1929   F T Everard (Greenhithe) (30/1/1929)

Champion barge on Thames and Medway on many occasions, rigged for racing, broken up at Greenhithe in 1964, Registry closed.

Sailing Barge, *Scot*

Off. No. 112845   Port of Registry London (No.76 in 1901)

Built Greenhithe, Kent, 1901, by F T Eberhardt

Net Tonnage: 60   Gross Tonnage: 76   Dead Weight: 130 tons to sea

Rig, Topsail, Type, Coasting Dimensions 85 feet x 19.7 feet x 6.1 feet

Original Owner: Wm T Clifford (City of London)

By 1910   F T Everard (5/4/1910)

Voyage 13/7/1934 London to Gt Yarmouth with Bagged Rice, Master J 'Knocker' Hart, at 3.15pm in collision with MV *England*, crew of 3 safe, barge sank in Harwich Harbour, Total Loss, wreck blown up, Registry closed 5/8/1936.

The Everard mule rigged coaster *Scotia* makes a fine sight under full canvas. When twenty-six years old, she was lost when driven ashore at Gt Yarmouth in 1929.

Sailing Barge *Scotia*

Off. No. 118364   Port of Registry London (No.189 in 1903)

Built Greenhithe, Kent, 1903, by F T Eberhardt

Net Tonnage: 77   Gross Tonnage: 109   Dead Weight: 180 Tons to sea

Rig, Mule, Type, Coasting   Dimensions 89.6 feet x 22.9 feet x 7.1 feet

Original Owner: F T Eberhardt (Greenhithe)

By 1917   F T Everard (Greenhithe)

Voyage 6/10/1929 Keadby to Maldon with 180 tons Basic Slag, Master T Willis, drove ashore at Gt Yarmouth in gale, crew of two saved by Lifeboat, 7/10/1929 total wreck, Registry closed 7/3/1930.

Sailing Barge, *Sirdar*

Off. No. 110033   Port of Registry London (No.248 in 1898)

Built Ipswich, Suffolk, 1898, by H Shrubsall

Net Tonnage: 53   Gross Tonnage: 72   Dead Weight: 125 Tons

Rig, Topsail (stackie)   Dimensions 84.8 feet x 19.4 feet x 5.8 feet

Original Owner:	H Shrubsall
By 1902	E A Hibbs (Brightlingsea)
By 1919	Owen Parry (Colchester)
By 1932	London & Rochester Trading Company

Took part in Thames and Medway Matches between 1956 and 1963, Thames and Medway Champion Barge, Engines fitted 1963 and used for passenger carrying/corporate hospitality, cruising only; 1976 hulked at Bedlams Bottom, Kent.

Sailing Barge *Spencer, ex Kent*

Off. No. 114755   Port of Registry London (No.189 in 1900)

Built Sweden, 1900, by Bergquava Syndicate/English Timber Company

Net Tonnage: 64   Gross Tonnage: 78   Dead Weight: 142 Tons

Rig, Gaff as built, changed to Topsail   Dimensions 83.8 feet x 19.8 feet x 5.6 feet

Original Owner:	Bergquava Syndicate (London, Broad Street, City)
By 1906	Mrs Susan A Eberhardt (Greenhithe)
By 1911	F T Everard (23/3/1911)

NB Built with caulked sides, 1946 hulk, 1949 Registry closed, broken up.

Tug *Sun XI*

Off. No. 148618   Port of Registry London

Built Hull, Humberside, 1925, by Earle's Company   Steel construction

Net Tonnage: 63   Gross Tonnage: 183   Engine: 112 HP

Original Owner:	W H J Alexander Limited (Gravesend)
By 1964	Schelde Towage, Antwerp, name changed to *Schelde X*

In 1965 sold to new owners in Sardinia and renamed *Andrea*; scrapped 1985.

Tug *Sun XII*

Off. No. 148637   Port of Registry London

Built Hull, Humberside, 1925, by Earle's Company   Steel construction

Net Tonnage: 63   Gross Tonnage: 183   Engine: 112 HP

Original Owner:	W H J Alexander Limited (Gravesend)
By 1969	Sold for scrap to shipbreakers, Belgium.

Identical twins, the London River tugs Sun XI and Sun XII, between them giving over 80 years service to W H J Alexander Limited.

Sailing Barge *Thames*
Off. No. 82883   Port of Registry London (No.68 in 1881)
Built Greenhithe, Kent, 1881, by A Keep
Net Tonnage: 45   Gross Tonnage: 49
Type, River; Rig, Topsail   Dimensions 80.5 feet x 17.9 feet x 5.4 feet
Original Owner: A Keep (City)
By 1912   J Rayfield (Northfleet)
Dumb barge, Registry closed 1916.

Clipper Ship *Thermopylae*
Built Clyde, Scotland, 1868, by Hood to design of Bernard Waymouth
Net Tonnage: 948   Gross Tonnage: 991   Underdeck: 927 Tons
Type, Tea Clipper   Dimensions 210 feet x 36 feet x 21 feet
Original Owner: (George Thompson) Aberdeen White Star Line
By 1890   Rice Milling Company (£5,000)
Made many fast passages with coal, tea and wool and was always compared with the marginally smaller *Cutty Sark*; from 1890 trading between Hong Kong and Victoria, British Columbia. Sold in 1895 to the Portuguese Government for use as a training vessel and renamed *Pedro Nunez*; on 13/10/1907 towed out of port and given 'Naval Funeral' and sunk at sea.

Sailing Barge *Tollesbury*
Off. No. 110315   Port of Registry Ipswich (originally Ramsgate)
Built Sandwich, Kent, 1901, by W Felton
Net Tonnage: 70   Gross Tonnage: 87   Dead Weight: 160 Tons to sea when new, later 150
Rig, Topsail, Type, Coasting
Original Owner: Frost (Tollesbury, Essex) (£550)
By 1912   R & W Paul (Ipswich)
Hull sheathed in 1927; 31/5/1940 towed by tug *Sun XII* with SB *Ethel Everard* to Dunkirk, arrived 0100 hours 1/6/1940, Master L Webb. Unloaded small arms, ammunition, dynamite and food for retreating British Expeditionary Force, later under attack by German aircraft for hours whilst anchored off with no wind and foul tide. *Tollesbury* towed back to England by tug *Cervia* with 270 troops on board, Captain Henry Miller of SB *Royalty* assisting; By 1950 Ruston diesel engine installed; 1978 houseboat at Pin Mill, Suffolk, late 1980s/early 1990s rebuilt at Ipswich, moved on completion to London Docklands for use as bar/diner, still in service 2001.

Sailing Barge *Veronica*
Off. No. 120691   Port of Registry London (No.54 in 1906)
Built East Greenwich, 1906, by H Shrubsall
Net Tonnage: 54   Gross Tonnage: 67.41   Dead Weight: 130 tons - advertisement
Rig, Topsail (stackie) Dimensions 85 feet x 19.15 feet x 6.65 feet
Original Owner: Clem W Parker (Bradwell)
By 1932   F T Everard (Greenhithe) (for £160)
By 1953 hulked at White Hart causeway, Greenhithe, awash every tide
1954/55 Extensive repairs and re-rig on Everard Yard, Greenhithe, for racing. Took part in Thames and Medway Matches, sailed by Jack Nunn, between 1956 and 1963, Thames and Medway Champion Barge; by 6/1966 houseboat at Chatham, owner Frank Kennedy, renamed *Veronica Belle*, derelict 1975. Hulked Bedlams Bottom, Kent.

Training Ship *Worcester, ex Frederick William*

Commenced building Portsmouth, Hampshire, 1864

Tonnage: 3,240   Dimension: 214 feet   Cost: £166,000

Almost the last of the 'Wooden Walls', sail Ship-of-the-Line; laid down as *Royal Sovereign* in 1833; in 1839 still under construction, name changed to *Royal Frederick*, still on building slip twenty years later when converted to steam powered auxiliary with 500 HP engines installed; launched a year later as *Frederick William*. Loaned to Worcester Management Committee, arrived Greenhithe 24/2/1877, used as Cadet Training Ship for Merchant Marine young officers until WWII; Towed away to be scrapped 11/1945.

Sailing Barge *Whitwell*

Off. No. 45338   Port of Registry Yarmouth (No.14 in 1864), London (No.187 in 1882)

Built Yarmouth, Norfolk, 20/5/1864, by Beeching

Net Tonnage: 62   Gross Tonnage: 71   Dead Weight: 160 tons - advertisement

Rig, Topsail, Type, Coasting Dimensions 86.2 feet x 21.2 feet x 6.3 feet

Original Owner: Not recorded

By 1882   A H Keep

By 1921   T Scholey & Company

By 1925   Prizeman (Leadenhall Street, London)

Registry closed 1929, derelict, broken up.

R & W Paul's *Tollesbury* seen here at the top of Ipswich dock, by then complete with wheelhouse and auxiliary power, though retaining a full staysail sailplan.

Picture Sources

The vast majority of the illustrations included are from photographs and postcards collected by Tony Farnham over many years. The following list is an attempt to reflect the sources of these where known, by page number and position:

Front Cover: F T Everard & Sons Ltd,
    K S Garrett collection
3: Gravesend Reporter
8: C & D Bristow, Miller family collection
10: Post Card
13: B T Pearce collection
14 top: Post Card, The Wykeham Collection
14 lower: Russell's Gravesend Brewery Ltd.
15: F C Gould, Gravesend, Kent
16: Guildhall Library, City of London
17: French Post Card, P.H. & Companie, Nancy
18 top: Post Card, J Beagles & Co. Ltd.
18 lower: Post Card, J Beagles & Co. Ltd.
19 top: Post Card, J Beagles & Co. Ltd.
19 lower: George Washington Wilson photo,
    Light Impressions, Liverpool
20: F T Everard & Sons Ltd,
    K S Garrett collection
21 top: Mick Twyman collection
21 lower: E J Carter Collection, Lincolnshire
    County Council, Gainsborough Library
22 top: Bexley Libraries & Museums
22 lower: Leslie G Arnold, ARPS, Leigh on Sea
23: F T Everard & Sons Ltd,
    K S Garrett collection
24: Mick Twyman collection
25: National Maritime Museum, London
26: R W Smith collection
27: Post Card
28 top: Post Card, Thornton Bros, Brompton, Kent
28 lower: Post Card
30: John Topham, Edenbridge, Kent
31: Walter Dowsett collection

32: A Duncan, Isle of Wight
33: G A Osbon
34: Walter Dowsett collection
35 top: German Propaganda Photograph
35 lower: German Propaganda Photograph,
    K S Garrett collection
36: Post Card, Elgenopname van Laarmans
37: Post Card
38: Chris Alston collection
39: Conway Picture Library
40 top: F C Gould, Gravesend, Kent, original,
    copy by Willis, Chatham, Kent
40 lower: F C Gould, Gravesend, Kent
42: Eric Watt collection
44: Kentish Times
45 top: Gravesend Reporter
45 lower: Kentish Times
51: John Reynolds collection
60: Post Card
62: Wilf Middleton collection
65: Post Card, F T Everard & Sons Ltd
68: E J Carter Collection, Lincolnshire
    County Council, Gainsborough Library
73 left: Walter Dowsett collection
73 right: Conway Picture Library,
    R-H Perks collection
74: National Maritime Museum, London
75 left: A Duncan, Isle of Wight
75 right: A Duncan, Isle of Wight
77: R & W Paul Ltd, R W Smith collection
Back Cover top: Gravesend Reporter
Back Cover lower: R-H Perks collection